Delicious
Under Pressure

Meredith Laurence

Photography by Jessica Walker

Walah!, LLC Publishers
Philadelphia

First Edition

Copyright © 2015 by Meredith Laurence.

Published in the United States by Walah!, LLC/Publishers

walah@me.com

Library of Congress Cataloging-in-Publication Data

    Laurence, Meredith.
       Delicious under pressure / Meredith Laurence ;
    photography by Jessica Walker. -- First edition.
       pages cm
       Includes index.
       At head of title: Blue jean chef.
       ISBN-13: 978-0-9827540-0-9
       ISBN-10: 0-9827540-0-0

       1. Pressure cooking. 2. Cooking, American. 3. Cookbooks.
    I. Title. II. Title: Blue jean chef delicious under pressure.

    TX840.P7L383 2015   641.5'87
                     QBI15-600116

Printed in USA

Book design by Janis Boehm
www.bound-determined.com

Photography by Jessica Walker
www.jessicawalkerphotography.com

Food styling by Bonne Di Tomo, Lisa Ventura and Lynn Willis

Acknowledgements

Writing a cookbook is never a solo project and I have many people to thank for helping me put this collection of recipes together.

Thank you to...

...Eric Theiss for unwavering support and for keeping my work life going when I was buried with recipe writing.

...to Janis Boehm for her friendship and beautiful book design. Just working with Janis makes me want to write more cookbooks!

...to Jessica Walker whose photos make me proud and hungry all at the same time.

...to Lisa Ventura for her help testing, tweaking, tasting and then making everything beautiful.

...to Bonne di Tomo and Lynn Willis, two of the hardest-working and talented people I know who make photo shoots a lot of fun.

...to Penny Markowitz for her keen eye on my writing, catching my shortcomings and offering suggestions.

I'm thrilled to call all of you friends!

And especially...to my perfect family...

...to Ruby, my adorable and not-so-critical taster. She loved every single recipe!

...to Sadie, my loyal and loving companion who has her nose in everything I do.

...to Annie Symes who stands by and supports me every step of the way in every part of my life. This book was no exception – you deserve a byline! I couldn't have done it without you - you helped keep me sane when all was crazy.

Forward
David Venable

It was 2001 when I met Blue Jean Chef Meredith Laurence for the first time. She had moved to Pennsylvania to host a show on QVC designed to help home cooks be better in the kitchen. She also worked with the program hosts and taught basic cooking classes. In no time at all, I became Meredith's student...and friend. She has always had an incredible passion for food and makes every recipe and technique seem so very, very easy.

Meredith wrote her first pressure-cooking cookbook in 2012 and I bought it. If anyone could teach me a thing or two about pressure cooking, Meredith could—and she did. When I heard she was writing a second pressure-cooking cookbook, I was thrilled! Having sold thousands of pressure cookers on QVC, I know foodies everywhere are hungry for two things: first, they need someone to share and teach the basics of pressure cooking; and second, they need delicious, easy-to-follow recipes. Meredith delivers BIG on both points in her new title. This book makes sense from the introduction to the index, and you'll feel as if Meredith is right beside you in your own kitchen showing you the way!

When I first sat down to take a peek at this book, I got about 50 pages in and then ran to the grocery store for ingredients to make her Sweet Vidalia Onion Joes recipe (which was OUT OF THIS WORLD). Every mouthwatering page is full of the most wonderful food...and all of it can be cooked so quickly. From meats and pastas to vegetarian specialties and breakfast dishes—and did I mention desserts?—there's something for every appetite. Wait until you see soups like Loaded Baked Potato, pastas like Creamy Tomato Macaroni, entrées such as Beef Brisket with Onion and Mushroom Gravy, and desserts like Peanut Butter Cheesecake. Your family will be overjoyed at dinnertime and you'll truly appreciate Meredith's variety and down-to-earth instruction.

So, enjoy this pressure-cooking roadmap that leads to some truly amazing meals. Come along with Meredith in her quest to make you even more comfortable in the kitchen and join me in busting out plenty of Pressure-Cooking Happy Dances!

David Venable
*QVC's Resident Foodie & Host of **In The Kitchen with David**®*

About this Book

I wanted this book and the recipes in it to be accessible to everyone. You'll find basic recipes here for the newcomer, as well as slightly more challenging recipes for those who want to take their pressure-cooking to the next level. I believe that every recipe in this book is something anyone can make, but I've marked those recipes that are really easy with a "Super Easy" stamp.

In addition, I wanted to make sure that there are lots of options for all kinds of cooks in the book and so I included a whole chapter of vegetarian main dishes. You will also find vegetarian recipes throughout many of the other chapters as well. All these recipes are marked with a "Vegetarian" stamp so you can quickly identify them. I also added a breakfast chapter and some glorious desserts to suit every occasion. Finally, I want you to know what my favorite recipes from the book are and I've marked those as "BJC Fav's".

The recipes in this book were tested with various electric pressure cookers, ranging from five quarts to ten quarts in size. Every recipe is guaranteed to work in a 6-quart or bigger pressure cooker. If your pressure cooker is smaller than five quarts, or if you are using a stovetop pressure cooker, take a look at the section Converting Recipes on page 16.

Table of Contents

Acknowledgements 5

Foreward 7

About this Book 8

Introduction 13

If You are Brand New to Pressure Cooking… 14

Converting Recipes 16

General Tips for Pressure Cooking 18

Recipe Rules 20

Soups and Chilies

Chicken and Corn Chowder 24

★■ French Canadian Yellow Split Pea Soup with Maple Cream 27

Chicken Noodle Soup 28

Curried Butternut Squash Pear Soup 29

Ginger Broth with Salmon and Shrimp 30

■★ Avglolemono with Chicken and Rice 32

■▼ Spicy Quinoa and Red Lentil Soup 33

▼ Cauliflower Cheddar Soup 35

★ Tortilla Soup 37

■ Loaded Baked Potato Soup 38

▼ Curried Carrot Soup with Apple and Almond Topping 41

Caribbean Pork Chili with Pineapple Salsa 42

▼ Black Bean and Mushroom Chili 44

Annie's Beef Chili 45

▼ Quinoa Chili with Kidney Beans and Corn 47

■ Chile Verde 48

Pasta

★■▼ Creamy Tomato Macaroni 52

■ Farfalle Putanesca 54

■▼ Spinach and Cheese Ravioli with Zucchini and Marinara 55

Fusilli with Hot Italian Sausage, Tomatoes, Arugula and Olives 57

Pasta Primer 58

Chili Macaroni 59

Turkey Tetrazzini 60

Lamb Bolognese with Pistachio-Gremolata 61

■ Penne Carbonara 63

■▼ Roasted Red Pepper Rigatoni with Feta Cheese 64

Turkey Bolognese Rigatoni 65

★■ Cavatappi con Vongole 66

Sunday Gravy 69

Poultry

★ Chicken and Lemon-Chive Dumplings 72

Greek Chicken and Potatoes 74

Chicken Marsala Stew with Mushrooms, Peas and Potatoes 75

■ Honey Mustard Chicken with Orange and Rosemary Potatoes 76

■ Salsa Chicken Thighs with Rice 79

Chicken Scoop 80

★■ Lemon Oregano Chicken Breasts with Orzo, Olives and Feta Cheese 81

Chicken Pot Pie with Leeks and Lemon 82

★■ Chicken Tikka Masala 85

Turkey Breast with Spinach, Feta, Lemon and Walnut Stuufing 88

Turkey Breast with Italian Sausage and Dried Cherry Stuffing 88

★ BBQ Turkey Mushroom Meatloaf 89

★ Blue Jean Chef Favorites   ■ Super Easy Recipes   ▼ Vegetarian

Table of Contents

Beef

Beef Brisket with Onion and Mushroom Gravy	92
■ Beef Brisket with Dried Plums, Cognac and Cream	94
★■ Parmesan Meatballs and Marinara	95
Corned Beef Reuben Casserole	97
Beef Braciola with Mushrooms	98
■ Sweet Vidalia Onion Joes	100
Turkish Beef and Eggplant Moussaka	101
★ Jiggs Dinner	103
Hunter's Beef Stew	104
★■ Beef Dip Sandwiches	107
Beef Bites	108
Stout-Braised Beef Short Ribs	109
Curried Beef with Cucumber Yogurt Sauce	110
Chipotle Pot Roast with Spicy Cannellini Beans	113

Pork

Pork Chops with Orange Marmalade Glaze	116
★ Dry-Rubbed Baby Back Ribs with BBQ Sauce	119
Dry-Rubbed Baby Back Ribs with Cherry Chipotle Sauce	120
Dry-Rubbed Baby Back Ribs with Sweet and Sour Sauce	120
Pork Report	121
★ Country Style Pork Ribs with Mustard and Cream	122
Pork Stew with Cabbage and Tomatoes	123
★ Pork Carnitas	125
★ Pot Roast Shoulder of Pork with Apple Gravy	126
■ Keilbasa and Sauerkraut and Apples	127
★■ Madeira Ham with Apricots	128
Pork Chops with Artichokes, Capers, Sundried Tomatoes and Lemons	131

Fish and Seafood

★ Provençal Fish Stew with Fennel and Potatoes	134
Calamari Stew	136
Lime Shrimp and Spicy Tomato Grits	137
★ Veracruz Style Snapper with Rice	139
Fish Facts	140
■ Salmon Putanesca with White Beans	141
Thai Coconut Mussels	142

Vegetarian Main Dishes

■▼ Risotto with Shiitake Mushrooms, Butternut Squash and Peas	146
▼ Lemon-Basil Ricotta Dumplings	148
■▼ Broccoli Rice Casserole	149
▼ Miso Brown Rice Bowl with Tofu and Edamame	151
★▼ Spaghetti Squash with Leek and Olive Marinara	152
■▼ Vegetable and Bean Stuffed Peppers with Marinara	154
▼ Vegetable Couscous with Tomatoes, Feta and Basil	155
★▼ Vegetarian Portobello Mushroom and Zucchini Moussaka	157
▼ Lentil and Chickpea Stew with Spicy Bitter Greens	158
▼ Vegetable Coconut Curry	159
★▼ Tadka Dal (Split Red Lentils) with Potatoes	160
▼ Beetroot Bourguignon with Fingerling Potatoes and Lentils	163

★ Blue Jean Chef Favorites   ■ Super Easy Recipes   ▼ Vegetarian

Grains and Beans

★▼ Farro Salad with Hazelnuts, Arugula, Grapes 166
Spill the Beans 168
Hoppin' John (or Black-Eyed Peas with Rice) 169
■▼ Quinoa Rice with Almonds 170
▼ Mexican Brown Rice with Corn and Chilies 171

■▼ Saffron Rice with Chickpeas 172
Smoky Bacon Tomato Chickpeas 174
■▼ Quinoa and Lentils with Mango and Mint 175
▼ Brown Rice Salad with Artichoke Hearts, Avocado and Pinenuts 176

Vegetable Side Dishes

★■▼ Cauliflower with Breadcrumbs and Lemon-Caper Vinaigrette 180
■▼ Creamy Maple Sweet Potatoes 182
■▼ Butternut Squash Purée with Orange and Honey 183
★ Beets and Potatoes with Bacon 185
■▼ Parsnip, Pear and Rosemary Mash 186
▼ Potato Gratin 189

■▼ Steamed Artichokes 190
▼ Roasted Red Pepper Aïoli 192
Tuna-Caper Aïoli 192
▼ Chipotle Orange Aïoli 192
Let's Veg 193
▼ Cumin Carrots with Kale 195

Breakfast

■ Ham and Cheddar Grits 198
■▼ Quinoa Porridge with Banana, Apricots and Almonds 200
■▼ Steel-Cut Oats with Apple and Raisins 201
★▼ Blueberry Polenta with Bananas and Maple Syrup 203
Breakfast Risotto with Bacon, Eggs and Tomatoes 204

■▼ Tropical Morning Rice Pudding 205
Compotes for pancakes and more...
▼ Blackberry Pear Compote 206
■▼ Strawberry Pomegranate Compote 208
▼ Maple Apple Blueberry Compote 209

Desserts

★ Chocolate Raspberry Almond Torte 212
Crème Caramel with Orange and Hazelnuts 215
Blackberry Croissant Bread Pudding 216
Brown Sugar Bourbon Bread Pudding 217
★ Banana Cake with Chocolate Chunks 218
Carrot Cake with Cream Cheese Icing 220

■ White Chocolate Raspberry Rice Pudding 221
■ Carrot Cake Rice Pudding 223
★ Pudding Chômeur 224
★ Lemon Blueberry Cheesecake 227
Peanut Butter Cheesecake 228
Cherry Cheesecake with Dark Chocolate Ganache 231

Recipe Index 232
Tip Index 238
Cooking Time Charts 239

Introduction

As all of our lives get busier, with more things to do and more devices to help us get things done, there seems to be less and less time to put a delicious meal on the table. And yet, eating, spending time together as a family, and enjoying a meal is still critically important to our well-being and day to day lives. So, it makes perfect sense that pressure-cooking is rapidly becoming more popular of late and a pressure cooker is turning into one of our essential kitchen tools.

Still, so many cooks only know how to make the traditional meals in a pressure cooker, rather than understanding how to bring it to its full potential and make truly delicious meals in one third of the time it would normally take with traditional cooking methods. That's my goal with this book – to help you understand pressure-cooking and show you how to make great dinners, lunches, or even breakfasts quickly and efficiently without compromising for a second on quality and taste.

As the Blue Jean Chef, I aim to make people as comfortable in the kitchen as they are in their blue jeans, and what could make a cook more comfortable than being able to pull a delicious meal out of one pot after simply setting a timer? If you're intimidated by pressure-cooking, I'm glad you picked up this book. It is my intention to make you comfortable and actually enjoy using your pressure cooker. If you've been pressure-cooking for a while and are bored with what you've been making, I'm glad you picked up this book. I'll show you how to make more interesting meals and get you to branch away from the same old stews, soups and chilies that you've been making. No matter what type of cook you are, get your new pressure cooker out of its box, or dust off your old pressure cooker, and get ready to make delicious meals under pressure.

If You are Brand New to Pressure Cooking...

Pressure Cooker Basics

A pressure cooker is a cooking vessel with a lid that locks on and prevents steam from escaping. As a result, the steam builds up pressure in the pressure cooker – about 12 to 15 pounds per square inch of pressure (psi) – and the temperature inside the cooker increases. At sea level, water boils at 212° F before it is converted into steam, and it cannot get any hotter than that, regardless of the heat source below it. In a pressure cooker, with 15 psi of pressure added, water boils at 250° F before being converted into steam. That means that we are able to cook foods inside a pressure cooker at higher temperatures, and they are therefore finished sooner – in about one third of the time it would take to cook on a regular stovetop. The time saved by using a pressure cooker is obviously a huge benefit, but that is secondary to how your foods taste out of the pressure cooker.

In a pressure cooker, the lid is sealed onto the pot letting nothing escape, and the flavors of the foods have nowhere to go but to mingle with each other. With flavor infused throughout, soups, stews, chilies, everything is intensely flavorful. Cuts of meat that usually need a long cooking time in order to become tender are transformed into spoon-tender, succulent meals. Because the lid prevents steam from escaping, foods remain moist too. The results of pressure-cooking are juicy, tender, moist and flavorful meals. All of that in one-third of the time it would normally take. You can't beat that!

Health Benefits

There are also health benefits to pressure-cooking. The main cooking medium in pressure-cooking is liquid rather than fat. When pressure-cooking, you can choose to almost eliminate fats, creating lean meals. Vegetables can be steamed quickly, retaining their crunch, color and nutrients.

Energy Efficient

Because it saves time and cooks foods faster, pressure cookers use up less energy than traditional methods of cooking. Also, because the steam and heat are trapped in the pressure cooker, you will find that your kitchen remains cooler. I love this for the summer months. With a pressure cooker, you have the versatility to cook foods all year round that you might otherwise reserve just for the winter.

Safe and Easy to Use

Pressure-cooking is also safe and easy. Most recipes call for you to start by browning foods either in the cooker itself or on the stovetop. Then, you combine the food with at least one to one and a half cups of liquid (check your pressure cooker manual for the minimum liquid requirement), lock the lid in place and set a timer. Electric pressure cookers do all the monitoring of time and temperature for you, so all you have to do is wait for the time to expire. There are safety valves built in to control for any unplanned occurrence and the locks on the machines prevent you from making a mistake and opening the unit when there's pressure inside. The horror stories of pressure cookers blowing up are truly tales of the past.

One of my favorite aspects of pressure-cooking is waiting for the timer to ring. I always have enough time to clean up the kitchen and set the table, which means that after dinner, I only have one pot and a few plates to clean.

Combining Pressure-Cooking with Other Cooking Techniques

Pressure-cooking can be your sole cooking method, or it can just speed up the process of making a meal combined with a different cooking technique. Ribs, for example, can be cooked in the pressure cooker and then popped onto the grill and brushed with BBQ sauce with an excellent result. Hams can be cooked in the pressure cooker and then glazed under the broiler for easy and beautiful browning.

Browning First

For visual appeal as well as for flavor, it's important to brown your foods either before pressure-cooking, or after the food has been cooked. Many electric pressure cookers now have BROWN settings, which will allow you to sear foods before you add the liquid required for cooking. If your electric pressure cooker does not have a BROWN setting, simply brown the foods on the stovetop in a skillet first, add the liquid to the skillet to deglaze the pan and scrape up any brown bits that have formed on the bottom from searing the meat, and pour the entire thing into the pressure cooker along with the remaining ingredients. It's a small step that does take a little time, but it is important to the final result.

Releasing Pressure

There are two ways to release the pressure in a pressure cooker. The first way is called the natural release method. This involves simply turning your electric pressure cooker off. The temperature will slowly decrease in the cooker and the pressure will come back to normal. Understand that a natural pressure release can take as long as fifteen minutes, so account for that time in your meal planning. Use the natural release method for meats in order to obtain the most tender results, for beans whose skins tend to burst otherwise, and for dishes with a lot of liquid where the liquid might spit out of the pressure release valve.

The alternative method to release the pressure in a pressure cooker is called the quick-release method. Electric pressure cookers have a release valve that you can turn to release the pressure manually. Steam will escape out of the valve until the pressure has returned to normal. Use the quick-release method for foods that are easily over-cooked, like grains, seafood or vegetables.

Converting Recipes

Converting From Traditional Recipes

Converting traditional recipes into pressure cooker recipes is easy. First step is to make sure you have one to one and a half cups of liquid (check your pressure cooker manual for the minimum liquid requirement) included in the recipe. There is very little evaporation during pressure-cooking, so you don't want a lot of liquid, but you do need the minimum required to steam and build the pressure. The next step is to simply cook the dish for one third of the time called for in the original recipe. Finally, use the appropriate release method for whatever it is you are cooking. See the "Releasing Pressure" section on the previous page.

Converting From Slow Cooker Recipes

Converting slow cooker recipes into pressure cooker recipes is also easy. There is very little evaporation from either slow cookers or pressure cookers, so they tend to have similar liquid quantities. Make sure the recipe has at least one to one and a half cups of liquid (check your pressure cooker manual for the minimum liquid requirement) and then use the cooking charts on page 239 or a similar recipe from the book to determine the cooking time for your meal.

Converting to Stovetop Pressure Cookers

Stovetop pressure cookers get to pressure a little faster than electric pressure cookers and also drop their pressure a little faster than electric pressure cookers. Because of this, the actual cooking time of foods in a stovetop pressure cooker is shorter than when using an electric pressure cooker. However, stovetop pressure cookers often reach a higher pressure level than electric pressure cookers, so it almost evens out. You won't find much difference in the timing for many recipes, but if you are cooking big pieces of meat, beans or grains, reduce the cooking time by a couple of minutes for stovetop cookers.

Converting to Smaller Pressure Cookers

Converting recipes for different sizes of pressure cookers can be tricky, but it doesn't need to be. The rule of thumb about pressure cookers is that you need to have at least one to one and a half cups of liquid in the recipe. (Check your pressure cooker manual for the minimum liquid requirement.) That liquid is needed to create the steam that will then create the pressure in the cooker. So, if you are decreasing the recipe, divide all the ingredients equally and then take a look at what you're left with. If there is less than one cup of liquid, increase just the liquid to the minimum amount required and leave the other quantities alone. Understand that you will probably have more sauce with your finished dish, or the final result of your cooking will be wetter than intended, but you can simply either reduce the liquid by simmering the sauce after the cooking time, or just use less of the sauce on the plate.

Here are a few tips on converting recipes:

● First of all, if your cooker can handle the quantity specified in the recipe, why not make the full recipe and freeze any leftovers for another occasion?

● If the liquid involved in the recipe is in proportion to the solid ingredients (such as rice or grains), do not make less than what one cup of liquid will permit.

● If you are making a roast or stew, you can decrease the meat quantity, while keeping the sauce ingredient quantities the same. Then, just use less sauce when you serve the dish.

● Because flavors can be intense in a pressure cooker, cut back on flavoring ingredients like dried herbs and spices when you are converting a regular recipe to the pressure cooker.

Converting for High Altitudes

Anyone cooking at a high altitude knows that water boils at a lower temperature because of the decreased atmospheric pressure. This affects the pressure inside a pressure cooker as well. So, when using a pressure cooker at higher altitudes, increase the cooking time by 5% for every 1000 feet over 2000 feet above sea level.

General Tips for Pressure-Cooking

Preparing to pressure cook

- Always use at least one to one and a half cups of liquid (or the minimum amount of liquid suggested by your pressure cooker manufacturer). Unfortunately, this does NOT include canned tomatoes or prepared sauces like BBQ sauce. The liquid required needs to be watery, like juice, wine, stock, or water.

- Never fill your pressure cooker more than two-thirds full.

- For ingredients that foam or expand in the pressure cooker – like pasta, beans, grains, legumes and some fruit – be sure to only fill the cooker half full. It is also prudent to add a little oil to the cooker when cooking these ingredients to help prevent foaming.

- Check the gasket of your pressure cooker before each use, to make sure that it is clean and properly in place. The gasket can hold on to odors from cooking. Try washing it in a vinegar-water solution to keep it odor free.

- If you're in a rush and you still want to brown the meat before pressure-cooking, double up and use a second skillet on the stovetop as well as the pressure cooker to sear the meat. You'll get twice as much meat browned in the same amount of time.

- If your cooker does not have a specific "brown" setting, just turn the cooker on and do not cover with the lid. The element at the bottom of the cooker will engage and heat up and you'll be able to brown right in the cooker.

Setting and building the pressure

- 95% of all pressure cooker recipes call for HIGH pressure. If your pressure cooker doesn't have low-medium-high settings for pressure, you probably only have the high setting. Because so many cookers only have the high setting, you'll find all the recipes in this book use high pressure.

- Some pressure cookers use the metric measure of kilopascals (kPa) as the unit of pressure, rather than pounds per square inch (psi). HIGH pressure is usually 12 to 15 psi, which would be roughly 80 to 100 kPa. To convert from kPa to psi, multiply the number of kPa by 0.15.

- Remember that it takes time for the pressure cooker to build the pressure inside. Depending on what and how much food you are cooking, that time can be as much as fifteen minutes. Try to account for that time the same way you would account for the time it takes for your oven to pre-heat.

- If your pressure cooker doesn't seem to be coming to pressure it might be because you don't have enough liquid inside. Open it up and add more liquid before trying again.

- If you find that steam is escaping from around the rim of your pressure cooker, or through the pressure release valve, check that the valve is closed and give the lid a firm push down. Pushing down on the lid helps the gasket form a seal around the rim of the pressure cooker and the cooker should almost immediately stop releasing steam and come to pressure. I do this almost every time I use a pressure cooker to ensure accurate timing of the recipe. Once the machine has come to pressure, I walk away and let it do the rest of the work.

Releasing the pressure

- A natural release can take longer than you think it should, depending on what and how much food you have inside the cooker. My rule of thumb is to allow a natural release for fifteen minutes. After that, I will release any residual pressure with the quick-release method without any negative effects.

- If the steam releasing from your pressure cooker during a quick-release starts to spit and sputter liquid, close the valve and let the pressure drop naturally. You can also hold a kitchen towel above the pressure release valve to stop any splattering from messing up your cabinets.

- Be careful opening the lid of the pressure cooker. Even though the pressure will have dropped, the food inside will still be very hot and steam will be released.

Finishing touches

- Because you need liquid to create the steam needed to build pressure, you never thicken the sauce before cooking. Instead, thicken sauces once the cooking procedure is over. See page 108 for sauce thickening techniques.

- Let the food cool for at least 5 minutes before serving it. Foods become very hot in a pressure cooker and not only are they likely to burn you if you eat them too quickly, but the flavors need a little time to blend and settle before serving.

- Invest in accessories for your pressure cooker. It will expand your repertoire.

  - A rack that fits inside your pressure cooker is very important to have. I have two small racks about 5-inches long by 4-inches wide. These can be used in any combination to fit most pressure cookers.

  - A small 7-inch cake pan will fit inside most pressure cookers. You'll need this to cook all the bread puddings and cheesecakes.

  - A steamer basket is nice to have in a pressure cooker for steaming vegetables among other things.

- Rarely, but on occasion, you might experience a "blow out" with your pressure cooker. This is not a sign of a faulty cooker, but is in fact a safety mechanism. A "blow out" is when the steam will suddenly be released from the cooker usually from the side of the lid. It occurs when too much pressure has built up in the cooker. Let the pressure drop completely, open the lid, make sure all the valves are clean and try your recipe again.

Recipe Rules

In every cooking class I've ever taught, I try to set people up for success by setting some ground rules. Sounds strict, but it really isn't. I prefer to think of these rules as helpful hints.

First rule – read the recipe from start to finish before you begin cooking. This is critical in order to know if you have all the ingredients, as well as if you have enough time to complete the recipe. Don't forget to account for the time it takes to come to pressure, as well as the time it takes to release the pressure naturally.

Second rule – buy the very best ingredients you can. A finished dish can only taste as good as its ingredients.

Third rule – do your *mise en place.* This means do all your prep work first. Chop what needs to be chopped. Measure what needs to be measured. This makes cooking much less stressful and more relaxing. Of course, you can start a step of the recipe in the middle of doing your *mise en place* if that first step in the recipe requires some time. You'll know this because you will have read the recipe all the way through first!

Fourth rule – taste your food before you take it to the table. You'd be surprised how many people forget this step, but it's really important. You should always take a few seconds to taste the food and re-season it if necessary.

Specifics about Ingredients

- **Tomatoes.** I prefer to use canned whole tomatoes and then chop or crush them by hand. I think they taste better than canned diced or crushed tomatoes. So, when you see "1 (28-ounce) can tomatoes, chopped", that means a can of whole tomatoes, chopped by hand. (Of course, you can substitute canned diced tomatoes if you want or need to.) Unless other wise specified, add everything that comes in the can of tomatoes – tomatoes and their juice – to the recipe. Remember that tomatoes do not count as the minimum liquid required in order to build the pressure.

- **Onions, Garlic and Carrots.** Unless you enjoy eating the skin and peels of these vegetables, assume that they should always be peeled.

- **Potatoes.** I specify whether or not to peel the potatoes before using them in the recipes. If it doesn't say "peeled" that means wash the potatoes, but leave the skins on.

- **Peppers.** People have different tastes and capacities to handle spicy foods. Similarly, chili peppers have very different levels of spiciness, even within the same type of pepper. If you like spicy foods, feel free to leave the seeds in the peppers. If you do not like spicy foods, always seed the peppers before incorporating them into the recipe. I don't say one way or another what to do, but leave the decision up to you.

- **Wine.** Unless otherwise specified, use dry wines in the recipes rather than sweet wines. Whatever you do, do not use cooking wine, which is filled with sodium and does not add any good flavors to your finished dish.

- **Substitution for Wine.** If you don't want to cook with wine for whatever reason, there are a number of substitutions you can make. Just think about what will add the best flavor to your finished dish. For red wine, try beef, chicken or rich vegetable stock, cranberry, pomegranate or red grape juice, or some red wine vinegar. For white wine, try chicken or vegetable stock, white grape or apple juice, or some white wine vinegar or lemon juice.

- **Good quality stock and other ingredients.** Sometimes you will see instruction to use "good quality stock" rather than just stock, or "Parmigiano-Reggiano cheese" rather than just Parmesan cheese. While I strongly recommend using the very best ingredients all the time, sometimes an ingredient has extra importance in a recipe and absolutely must be of the highest quality. If you see "good quality", then you'll know that you can't substitute an inferior ingredient in its place and expect the same excellent results.

I may call them rules, but all of these points are just to set you off on the right path!

If you would like to learn more about pressure-cooking, or would like more recipes for your pressure cooker and other cooking tools, please visit me at www.bluejeanchef.com.

Soups
and
Chilies

Chicken and Corn Chowder
French Canadian Yellow Split Pea Soup with Maple Cream
Chicken Noodle Soup
Curried Butternut Squash Pear Soup
Ginger Broth with Salmon and Shrimp
Avglolemono with Chicken and Rice
Spicy Quinoa and Red Lentil Soup
Cauliflower Cheddar Soup
Tortilla Soup
Loaded Baked Potato Soup
Curried Carrot Soup with Apple and Almond Topping
Caribbean Pork Chili with Pineapple Salsa
Black Bean and Mushroom Chili
Annie's Beef Chili
Quinoa Chili with Kidney Beans and Corn
Chile Verde

Chicken and Corn Chowder

This is a great soup to have at the end of the summer when corn is still in season and you're looking forward to the fall. But, don't fret if you're craving corn chowder outside of corn season – you can use frozen kernels for this just as easily.

Serves
6

Cooking Time
8 Minutes

Release Method
Quick-release

2 tablespoons olive oil

1 onion, finely diced

3 ribs of celery, finely diced

1 red bell pepper, finely diced

2 cloves garlic, minced

3 cups fresh corn kernels or
1-pound bag frozen corn kernels

1 teaspoon dried thyme leaves

⅛ teaspoon crushed red pepper flakes

2 teaspoons salt

freshly ground black pepper

4 cups chicken stock

2 large chicken breasts, on the bone
but skin removed

1 cup heavy cream

1 tablespoon flour

¼ cup sliced scallions

1. Pre-heat the pressure cooker using the BROWN setting.

2. Add the oil and sauté the onion and celery for 3 to 4 minutes. Add the red pepper, garlic, corn kernels, thyme, crushed red pepper flakes, salt and black pepper and mix well, cooking for another minute or two.

3. Add the chicken stock and chicken breasts, and make sure the chicken is submerged in the liquid. Lock the lid in place.

4. Pressure cook on HIGH for 8 minutes.

5. Release the pressure using the QUICK-RELEASE method and carefully remove the lid. Remove the chicken to a side plate and let it cool slightly so that you can shred the chicken with your fingers. While the chicken cools, purée 2 cups of the soup using a blender or immersion blender. Return the puréed soup and the shredded chicken to the cooker and mix well.

6. Return the cooker to the BROWN setting, pour in the heavy cream and vigorously whisk in the flour. Season to taste with salt and pepper, and serve with chopped scallions on top.

A nice way to give this soup a little more pizzazz is to make your own croutons to go on top. Cut a few slices of Italian or multi-grain bread into large cubes, toss with olive oil, salt and pepper and toast in a 350ºF oven for about 10 to 15 minutes, or until nicely browned. This is also really nice with oyster crackers.

French Canadian Yellow Split Pea Soup with Maple Cream

This Quebeçois comfort food is different from the green split pea soup that I grew up with, but I love it and it couldn't be easier to make. The ham bone or smoked pork hock adds great flavor, but you can still make the soup without it if you don't have one or the other on hand. Of course, you would have a ham bone on hand if you made the Madeira Ham with Apricots (page128).

Serves
4 to 6

Cooking Time
10 Minutes

Release Method
Combo

1 tablespoon butter

1 onion, finely chopped

2 carrots, finely chopped

2 cloves garlic, smashed

4 sprigs fresh thyme

2 cups yellow split peas

1 ham bone or smoked pork hock, rinsed (optional)

12 ounces cooked ham, cut into large 3-inch chunks

2 bay leaves

6 cups water

½ cup sour cream

1 tablespoon maple syrup

salt and freshly ground black pepper, to taste

1. Pre-heat the pressure cooker using the BROWN setting.

2. Add the butter to the pressure cooker and sauté the onion, carrot, garlic and thyme. Cook until the vegetables just start to soften – about 5 minutes. Add the split peas, ham bone, ham chunks, bay leaves and the water. Lock the lid in place.

3. Pressure cook on HIGH for 10 minutes.

4. While the soup is cooking, combine the sour cream and maple syrup in a small bowl.

5. Let the pressure drop NATURALLY for 10 minutes. Then release any remaining pressure using the QUICK-RELEASE method and carefully remove the lid. Remove the ham hock from the pot and let it cool enough to pull any meat from the bone. Remove the chunks of ham and cut into small dice. Return the diced ham to the soup and season to taste with salt and freshly ground black pepper. Serve with a drizzle or dollop of the maple cream on top.

The maple cream in this recipe is also delicious on a butternut soup too.

Chicken Noodle Soup

Nothing makes you feel better when you have a rotten cold than a hot bowl of chicken noodle soup. The only trouble is that you rarely feel like making it when you most need it. Here's a way to get a homemade bowl of healing soup into your hands quickly!

Serves
6 to 8

Cooking Time
5 Minutes

Release Method
Quick-release

2 tablespoons olive oil

1 pound boneless skinless chicken breasts, cut into bite-sized pieces

1 pound boneless skinless chicken thighs, cut into bite-sized pieces

salt and freshly ground black pepper

1 onion, finely chopped

3 carrots, sliced ¼-inch thick

3 ribs celery, sliced ¼-inch thick

2 to 3 cloves garlic, smashed

1 teaspoon dried thyme

2 quarts good quality or homemade unsalted chicken stock

4 cups dry wide egg noodles (about 6 ounces)

4 sprigs fresh parsley, leaves picked and stems finely chopped

1. Pre-heat the pressure cooker using the BROWN setting.

2. Add the olive oil and brown the chicken pieces briefly, seasoning with salt and pepper. Add the onion, carrots, celery, garlic and thyme and cook for another 2 to 3 minutes. Pour in the stock and add the egg noodles. Season with salt and freshly ground black pepper and lock the lid in place.

3. Pressure cook on HIGH for 5 minutes.

4. Release the pressure using the QUICK-RELEASE method and carefully remove the lid. Season to taste again with salt and pepper and add the parsley to the soup when serving. (P.S. Don't forget to remove the garlic cloves!)

 Shortcut

If you're in a hurry, or don't feel up to it, skip the browning step and just put all the ingredients except for the parsley into the cooker and cook on HIGH for 7 minutes. Then return to step 4. The noodles will be a little extra soft, but they will still taste great.

Curried Butternut Squash Pear Soup

You can easily substitute any hard winter squash for the butternut squash in this recipe.
Try acorn, kabocha, buttercup, delicata or even pumpkin.

Serves
6

Cooking Time
8 Minutes

Release Method
Quick-release

2 tablespoons olive oil

1 onion, diced

1 to 2 teaspoons curry powder
(depending on your taste)

2 cups chicken stock

2 cups water

8 cups chopped butternut squash
(1 medium squash), diced (½-inch cubes)

2 pears, peeled and chopped

salt and freshly ground black pepper,
to taste

yogurt, for garnish

toasted hazelnuts, for garnish

1. Pre-heat the pressure cooker using the BROWN setting.

2. Add the olive oil and sauté the onion until it starts to soften - about 5 minutes. Add the curry powder and cook for another minute or two. Add the chicken stock, water, butternut squash, and pears and lock the lid in place.

3. Pressure cook on HIGH for 8 minutes.

4. Release the pressure using the QUICK-RELEASE method and carefully remove the lid. Purée the soup in batches using a blender (remembering not to fill the blender more than half full with the hot mixture), or all at one time in the pressure cooker insert with an immersion blender. Season to taste with salt and pepper, and thin the soup to the desired consistency with more water if necessary. Serve with a dollop of yogurt and a sprinkling of toasted hazelnuts.

If peeling and chopping butternut squash is not on your agenda, you can buy butternut squash already peeled and chopped at most grocery stores. That makes this soup a breeze and you'll be looking for something to do!

Ginger Broth
with Salmon and Shrimp

This delicately flavored soup is quick to make and can be a nice light starter for a dinner party. It's important to use a really good chicken stock, or if you can find a seafood stock, even better!

Serves
4 to 6

Cooking Time
1 Minute

Release Method
Quick-release

1 tablespoon vegetable oil

5 scallions - whites cut into thin strips (1½-inches long); greens sliced on the bias and reserved

1 large carrot, julienned

1 clove garlic, smashed

2-inch piece of fresh ginger, peeled and cut into very thin strips (1-inch long)

¼ teaspoon crushed red pepper flakes

3 ounces shiitake mushrooms, stems removed and caps thinly sliced (about 2 cups)

6 small white potatoes, scrubbed and sliced ¼-inch thin

6 cups good quality or homemade unsalted chicken stock

2 tablespoons soy sauce

10 ounces salmon, cut into 1-inch cubes

18 large frozen shrimp, partially thawed, peeled and deveined

1 lime, cut into wedges

1. Pre-heat the pressure cooker using the BROWN setting.

2. Add the oil and briefly sauté the scallion whites, carrot, garlic, ginger, crushed red pepper flakes and mushrooms for 2 to 3 minutes. Add the potatoes and chicken stock and lock the lid in place.

3. Pressure cook on HIGH for 1 minute.

4. Release the pressure using the QUICK-RELEASE method and carefully remove the lid. Stir in the soy sauce and place the salmon and shrimp into the hot broth. Cover immediately and let the soup sit for 6 to 8 minutes. This will be enough time and heat to cook the seafood and also give the soup time to cool to an edible temperature. Stir in the scallion greens and serve in bowls, seasoning to taste with more soy sauce and a squeeze of lime.

If you don't use fresh ginger very often in your cooking, store any leftover ginger in your freezer, wrapped in a sealable plastic bag with the air squeezed out. It should last up to 6 months that way. You can even grate it from frozen easily too!

Avglolemono with Chicken and Rice

I had a Greek math teacher in high school who used to make Avglolemono for her young daughters at their request. It's like the Greek equivalent to chicken noodle soup, but it has rice instead of noodles, is thickened with egg and seasoned with lemon juice. I'm not sure if it has the healing powers of chicken noodle soup, but I know that it's incredibly satisfying.

Serves
4

Cooking Time
8 Minutes

Release Method
Quick-release

2 tablespoons olive oil

1 onion, finely diced (about 1 cup)

1 cup long-grain rice

4 cups good quality or homemade unsalted chicken stock

2 chicken breasts, on the bone, but skin removed

2 eggs, lightly beaten

1 lemon, zest and juice

salt and freshly ground black pepper, to taste

¼ cup fresh parsley leaves

1. Pre-heat the pressure cooker using the BROWN setting.

2. Add the olive oil and sauté the onion until it starts to soften – about 5 minutes. Add the rice, stir well and cook for another minute or two. Add the chicken stock and chicken breasts, submerging them under the liquid. Lock the lid in place.

3. Pressure cook on HIGH for 8 minutes.

4. Release the pressure using the QUICK-RELEASE method and carefully remove the lid. Remove the chicken to a side plate and when cool enough to touch, pull the meat from the bone and chop into small pieces.

5. While the chicken cools, whisk the eggs in a bowl until frothy. Whisking constantly, add the lemon juice to the eggs and then add a ladle full of the hot broth. Whisk this mixture back into the hot pressure cooker. The soup should thicken nicely. Stir the chopped chicken back into the soup and season to taste with salt and freshly ground black pepper. Serve with some lemon zest and a few parsley leaves on top.

Did You Know...?

This soup will continue to get thicker as it sits or if kept as leftovers. You can thin it out to the right consistency with more chicken stock or water.

Spicy Quinoa and Red Lentil Soup

The funny thing about red lentils is that they turn yellow when cooked. I can't decide whether that's exciting or disappointing, but it is what it is. This soup is simple, with a spicy finish. The heat of chili peppers varies from pepper to pepper, so try a little sour cream to tame the heat if it's too intense.

Serves
4 to 6

Cooking Time
7 Minutes

Release Method
Quick-release

1 tablespoon olive oil

1 red chili pepper or Jalapeño pepper, sliced into rings

1 cup red lentils

1 cup quinoa

2 sprigs fresh thyme

2 teaspoons salt

3 cups water

3 cups vegetable or chicken stock

salt and freshly ground black pepper

sour cream, for garnish (optional)

1. Pre-heat the pressure cooker using the BROWN setting.

2. Add the olive oil and sauté the chili pepper for about 3 minutes. Add the red lentils, quinoa, thyme, salt, water and stock to the pressure cooker and lock the lid in place.

3. Pressure cook on HIGH for 7 minutes.

4. Release the pressure using the QUICK-RELEASE method and carefully remove the lid. Stir vigorously to smash some of the lentils. Season to taste with salt and freshly ground black pepper and serve.

Dress It Up

For an interesting garnish on this soup, toast some quinoa and sesame seeds in a skillet with a little oil, mix with chopped chives and sprinkle the mixture on top of the soup with a drizzle of olive oil.

Cauliflower Cheddar Soup

You'll want a good sharp Cheddar cheese for this soup to give it a pronounced flavor, so pick your favorite Cheddar and it's flavor will shine through.

Serves
4

Cooking Time
6 Minutes

Release Method
Quick-release

2 tablespoons butter

1 onion, chopped (1 cup)

1 clove garlic, smashed

1 teaspoon fresh thyme leaves

1 medium head of cauliflower, chopped

salt and freshly ground black pepper

2 cups chicken stock

2 cups grated sharp white Cheddar cheese

4 scallions, sliced on the bias

ground paprika or cayenne pepper, for garnish

1. Pre-heat the pressure cooker using the BROWN setting.

2. Add the butter, onion, garlic and thyme. Cook for 4 to 5 minutes, stirring occasionally. Add the cauliflower and season with salt and pepper. Pour in the chicken stock and lock the lid in place.

3. Pressure cook on HIGH for 6 minutes.

4. Release the pressure using the QUICK-RELEASE method and carefully remove the lid. Purée the soup in batches using a blender (remembering not to fill the blender more than half full with the hot mixture) or all at one time with an immersion blender. Return the soup to the cooker while it is still hot, add the cheese and stir until it has all melted. Season the soup again to taste with salt and pepper. Sprinkle the scallions and paprika on top and serve.

Don't feel like blending the soup? Give it a good stir with a wooden spoon and leave it chunky.

Tortilla Soup

This soup is a favorite of mine. I love Mexican flavors and this soup is like a burrito in a bowl minus the rice. I don't know about you, but I don't often have leftover or stale tortilla chips to use up in this soup, but you don't have to twist my arm to buy a new bag either!

Serves
4 to 6

Cooking Time
8 Minutes

Release Method
Quick-release

2 tablespoons olive oil

1 onion, finely diced

2 cloves garlic, minced

1 Jalapeño pepper, minced or sliced into rings

1 red bell pepper, chopped

1 tablespoon chili powder

1 teaspoon ground cumin

1 (28-ounce) can fire-roasted tomatoes, diced

3 cups good quality or homemade unsalted chicken stock

1 (15-ounce) can black beans, drained and rinsed

1 (15-ounce) can red kidney beans, drained and rinsed

2 boneless skinless chicken breasts

salt and freshly ground black pepper

4 cups (about 6 ounces) corn tortilla chips, broken into pieces

1 avocado, peeled and sliced

½ cup fresh cilantro leaves

½ cup grated Cheddar cheese

1. Pre-heat the pressure cooker using the BROWN setting.

2. Add the olive oil and sauté the onion until it starts to soften – about 5 minutes. Add the garlic, Jalapeño pepper, red pepper and spices, and cook for another minute or two. Add the tomatoes, chicken stock, beans and chicken breasts, submerging the chicken under the liquid. Lock the lid in place.

3. Pressure cook on HIGH for 8 minutes.

4. Release the pressure using the QUICK-RELEASE method and carefully remove the lid. Remove the chicken to a side plate and when cool enough to touch, shred the chicken with two forks into small pieces.

5. Return the chicken to the soup and season to taste with salt and freshly ground black pepper. Place some tortilla chips into each bowl and ladle the soup on top. Garnish with avocado, cilantro and Cheddar cheese.

You can use dried beans in this recipe if you prefer. Just cook the beans on their own first, covered in water on HIGH pressure for 5 minutes. Let the pressure drop naturally, drain the beans and then proceed with the recipe from the beginning.

Loaded Baked Potato Soup

Baked potato soup is usually made with leftover baked potatoes, but here we cook the potatoes quickly in the pressure cooker with their skins on. The skins of Yukon Gold potatoes are thin, but they give this soup a rustic taste. Load up your bowl the same way you load up your potato!

Serves
6 to 8

Cooking Time
6 Minutes

Release Method
Quick-release

½ pound bacon, chopped

3 pounds Yukon Gold potatoes, scrubbed and chopped (1-inch chunks)

4 cups water

1 tablespoon salt

freshly ground black pepper

½ cup heavy cream (optional)

sour cream, for garnish

grated Cheddar cheese, for garnish

chopped fresh chives or scallions, for garnish

1. Pre-heat the pressure cooker using the BROWN setting.

2. Add the bacon and cook until it starts to get crispy. Remove the bacon with a slotted spoon and set it aside. Add the potatoes and stir to coat in the bacon fat. Add the water, salt and pepper and lock the lid in place.

3. Pressure cook on HIGH for 6 minutes.

4. Release the pressure using the QUICK-RELEASE method and carefully remove the lid. Purée the soup in batches using a blender (remembering not to fill the blender more than half full with the hot mixture) or a food mill, or all at one time using an immersion blender until just smooth. Try not to over-blend the soup or it will become gluey. Add the heavy cream (if using), and season again to taste with salt and freshly ground black pepper. Thin the soup to the desired consistency with water if necessary (it will get thicker over time). Garnish as you would a baked potato, with sour cream, grated Cheddar cheese, chopped fresh chives or scallions and the cooked bacon.

Shortcut

If you don't want to blend the soup at the end, add another minute to the cooking time and give the soup a good stir with a wooden spoon to break the potato up. It will be chunky, but just as delicious.

Curried Carrot Soup
with Apple and Almond Topping

Different brands of curry powder have different flavors, and cooks will argue about which one is best until the cows come home. My suggestion is to just make sure your curry powder is not old – not passed down from your mother and not on its second decade in the back of your spice cupboard. If you don't use curry powder often, buy the smallest amount you can and try to use fresh curry powder whenever possible.

Serves
6 to 8

Cooking Time
8 Minutes

Release Method
Quick-release

1 tablespoon oil

1 tablespoon butter

1 onion, finely chopped

2 pounds carrots, sliced (4 to 5 cups)

2 teaspoons curry powder

4 cups vegetable stock

salt and freshly ground black pepper

1 Granny Smith apple, finely diced

½ cup coarsely chopped toasted almonds

chopped fresh chives, for garnish

1. Pre-heat the pressure cooker using the BROWN setting.

2. Add the oil and butter and sauté the onion and carrots until the onion starts to become tender - about 5 minutes. Stir in the curry powder and cook for another minute. Then add the vegetable stock and lock the lid in place.

3. Pressure cook on HIGH for 8 minutes.

4. While the soup is cooking, combine the apple, almonds and chives in a small bowl.

5. Release the pressure using the QUICK-RELEASE method and carefully remove the lid. Purée the soup in batches using a blender (remembering not to fill the blender more than half full with the hot mixture) or all at once with an immersion blender. Season to taste with salt and pepper. Sprinkle the apple-almond mixture on top of the soup as you serve it.

Grab a bag or two of baby cut carrots for this recipe, and you've saved yourself the peeling and chopping!

Caribbean Pork Chili with Pineapple Salsa

This "chili" is a fun mix of cuisines and makes a nice change from the usual chili. It's spicy like a chili, but has a hint of Caribbean flavors with the coconut milk and pineapple salsa. It's bright and fun - it's like a fiesta chili!

Serves
6 to 8

Cooking Time
20 Minutes

Release Method
Natural

2 tablespoons flour

salt and freshly ground black pepper

2½ to 3 pounds pork stew meat (1-inch cubes)

1 tablespoon vegetable oil

1 onion, diced

1 green bell pepper, diced

2 Jalapeño peppers, seeded and minced

1½ tablespoons chili powder

1 teaspoon dried oregano

2 teaspoons ground cumin

2 teaspoons salt

1 (28-ounce) can diced tomatoes

2 (15.5-ounce) cans chickpeas, drained and rinsed

½ cup coconut milk

½ cup chicken stock

1 (14-ounce) can refried beans

Pineapple Salsa:

1½ cups fresh pineapple, finely chopped

1 cup grape tomatoes, quartered

½ small red onion, finely chopped

½ red bell pepper, finely chopped

1 Jalapeño pepper, seeded and minced

2 tablespoons coconut milk

1 tablespoon cilantro

juice of ½ lime

1. Pre-heat the pressure cooker using the BROWN setting.

2. Combine the flour, salt and pepper and toss the pork cubes in the flour to coat. Add the oil to the cooker and brown the pork on all sides. Set the browned pork aside.

3. Add the onion and peppers to the cooker and sauté until they start to soften – about 5 minutes. Stir in the chili powder, oregano, cumin and salt, and return the browned pork to the cooker. Add the tomatoes, chickpeas, coconut milk and stock and stir well. Lock the lid in place.

4. Pressure cook on HIGH for 20 minutes.

5. While the chili is cooking, combine all the salsa ingredients in a bowl and season to taste with salt and freshly ground black pepper.

6. Let the pressure drop NATURALLY and carefully remove the lid. Stir the refried beans into the chili to thicken. Serve the chili in bowls, topped with the pineapple salsa.

Black Bean and Mushroom Chili

Button mushrooms, Crimini (brown) mushrooms and Portobello mushrooms are actually the same variety of mushroom, but at different stages of maturity. A white button mushroom is an immature version of a brown Crimini mushroom, which in turn is an immature version of a Portobello mushroom. I prefer the deeper, earthier flavor of brown mushrooms to white mushrooms, so that's what is called for here.

Serves
6 to 8

Cooking Time
3 + 8 Minutes

Release Method
Combo

2 cups dried black beans

2 tablespoons olive oil

1 onion, chopped

2 ribs celery, chopped

3 large cloves garlic, minced

2 red bell peppers, chopped

1 pound Portobello, Crimini or brown mushrooms, quartered or cut into chunks

1 teaspoon dried ground cumin

1 teaspoon dried oregano

2 tablespoons chili powder

1 tablespoon salt

2 tablespoons chopped Chipotle peppers in adobo

1 (28 ounce) can tomatoes, chopped

2 cups vegetable stock

¼ cup fresh cilantro or parsley

sour cream, lime wedges, grated Cheddar cheese (for garnish)

1. Place the beans in the pressure cooker and add enough water to cover the beans by one inch. Pressure cook on HIGH for 3 minutes. Let the pressure drop NATURALLY and carefully remove the lid. Drain the beans and set aside.

2. Pre-heat the pressure cooker using the BROWN setting.

3. Add the olive oil and sauté the onion, celery, and garlic until the onion starts to become tender – about 5 minutes. Add the peppers, mushrooms, spices and chipotle peppers and continue to cook for a few minutes. Add the tomatoes and vegetable stock, and return the beans to the pressure cooker. Lock the lid in place.

4. Pressure cook on HIGH for 8 minutes.

5. Let the pressure drop NATURALLY for 15 minutes. Then, release any residual pressure using the QUICK-RELEASE method and carefully remove the lid. Stir in the fresh cilantro or parsley. Serve with sour cream, lime wedges and Cheddar cheese.

If you decide to use Portobello mushrooms for this recipe, use a table spoon to scrape out the dark brown gills on the underside of the mushroom. While there's nothing wrong with eating the gills of the mushroom, they tend to make the finished dish very black in color – although that's not really an issue with this recipe either!

Annie's Beef Chili

The chili that Annie makes is a hit with everyone who tastes it! Here's a quick and easy version of Annie's chili to feed a crowd. There's a sweet note to this chili and its colorful ingredients make for a pretty bowl. Make a big batch – the leftovers freeze really well.

Serves
6 to 8

Cooking Time
10 Minutes

Release Method
Quick-release

1 pound lean ground beef

1 tablespoon vegetable oil

1 onion, chopped

2 ribs celery, chopped

8 ounces of button mushrooms, quartered

2 tablespoons chili powder

2 teaspoons salt

1 (10-ounce) can of cream of tomato soup (not condensed)

¼ cup ketchup

2 (28-ounce) can tomatoes, chopped

1½ cup beef or chicken stock

1 red bell pepper, chopped

1 green bell pepper, chopped

1 cup frozen corn kernels

1 (15-ounce) can red kidney beans, drained and rinsed

1 (15-ounce) can chickpeas (garbanzo beans), drained and rinsed

1. Pre-heat pressure cooker using the BROWN setting. Brown the beef and render out any fat. Once browned, remove the beef to a bowl with a slotted spoon and set aside. Drain off any fat remaining in the cooker.

2. Add the oil to the cooker and sauté the onion and celery until it starts to become tender – about 5 minutes. Add the mushrooms and cook for another 2 minutes. Add the chili powder and salt, and cook for another minute. Return the browned beef to the cooker along with all the remaining ingredients. Stir well and lock the lid in place.

3. Pressure cook on HIGH for 10 minutes.

4. Release the pressure using the QUICK-RELEASE method and carefully remove the lid. Season to taste again with salt and freshly ground pepper. Serve alone or over rice with any number of garnishes – cilantro, parsley, sour cream, grated Cheddar cheese, sliced Jalapeño peppers.

Quinoa Chili
with Kidney Beans and Corn

This is a delicious vegetarian chili! Quinoa is a complete protein – supplying all nine essential amino acids – and turns this into a chili that fills you up and keeps you full.

Serves
6 to 8

Cooking Time
4 + 10 Minutes

Release Method
Combo

1 cup dried kidney beans

2 tablespoons olive oil

1 onion, diced

3 cloves garlic, minced

2 red bell peppers, chopped

2 green bell peppers, chopped

1 Jalapeño pepper, sliced (leave the seeds in if you like a spicier chili)

1 teaspoon dried oregano

2 tablespoons chili powder

1 tablespoon salt

1 cup quinoa, rinsed

2 tablespoons tomato paste

1 (28-ounce) can tomatoes, chopped

4 cups vegetable stock

2 cups corn kernels (fresh, or frozen and thawed)

½ cup chopped fresh cilantro or parsley

sour cream and diced avocado
(for garnish)

1. Place the beans in the pressure cooker and add enough water to cover the beans by one inch. Pressure cook on HIGH for 4 minutes. Let the pressure drop NATURALLY and carefully remove the lid. Drain the beans and set aside.

2. Pre-heat the pressure cooker using the BROWN setting.

3. Add the oil and sauté the onion and garlic until the onion starts to become tender – about 5 minutes. Add the peppers and spices and continue to cook for a few minutes. Stir in the quinoa, tomato paste, tomatoes and stock. Return the beans to the cooker, stir and lock the lid in place.

4. Pressure cook on HIGH for 10 minutes.

5. Release the pressure using the QUICK-RELEASE method and carefully remove the lid. Stir in the corn kernels and let them heat through. Season to taste with salt and stir in the fresh cilantro or parsley. Serve with sour cream and diced avocado.

There are a number of easy ways to cut corn kernels off the cob. You can stand the ear of corn in a bowl and slice straight down the ear of corn catching the kernels in the bowl, or lay it flat on a cutting board and simply cut down the sides, rotating the ear around to cut off every side.

Chile Verde

Chili Verde is usually made with roasted tomatillos. Here we add a jar of tomatillo salsa, which includes other ingredients and spices that add flavor to the chili. The salsa has a huge role in this dish with respect to flavor and spiciness, so pick a salsa that suits your tastes.

Serves
6

Cooking Time
15 Minutes

Release Method
Natural

1 to 2 tablespoons vegetable oil

3 pounds pork butt or shoulder, trimmed of fat and cut into bite-sized pieces

salt, to taste

1 onion, rough chopped

2 Poblano peppers, diced

1 teaspoon dried oregano

½ teaspoon ground dried cumin

24 ounces jarred tomatillo salsa

1 cup chicken stock

¼ cup chopped fresh cilantro (or parsley)

1 cup sour cream

1. Pre-heat the pressure cooker on the BROWN setting.

2. Add one tablespoon of the oil and brown the pork pieces in batches, seasoning with salt and adding more oil as needed. Set the browned pork aside. Add the onion, Poblano pepper and spices and cook for another 5 minutes. Add the salsa and the chicken stock, return the pork to the cooker, stir well and lock the lid in place.

3. Pressure cook on HIGH for 15 minutes.

4. Let the pressure drop NATURALLY and carefully remove the lid. Season to taste again with salt and stir in the cilantro. Serve over rice and beans, or alone with a dollop of sour cream on top.

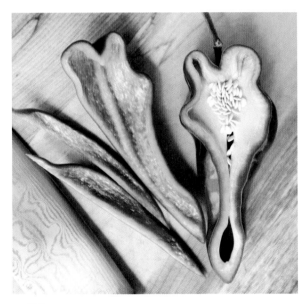

Poblano peppers are a mild flavored, dark green pepper. If you can't find Poblanos in your grocery store, use green bell peppers.

Pasta

Creamy Tomato Macaroni

Farfalle Putanesca

Spinach and Cheese Ravioli with Zucchini and Marinara

Fusilli with Hot Italian Sausage, Tomatoes, Arugula and Black Olives

Chili Macaroni

Turkey Tetrazzini

Lamb Bolognese with Pistachio Gremolata

Penne Carbonara

Roasted Red Pepper Rigatoni with Feta Cheese

Turkey Bolognese Rigatoni

Cavatappi con Vongole

Sunday Gravy

Creamy Tomato Macaroni

Creamy Tomato Macaroni (or tomato macaroni soup) is comfort food in Quebec to a certain generation. It was what you found at snackbars or roadside diners across the province. Simple and delicious, always buttery or creamy, it's bound to please everyone in the family.

Serves
4

Cooking Time
5 Minutes

Release Method
Quick-release

3 tablespoons butter

½ cup finely diced onion

½ cup finely diced celery

1 garlic clove, smashed

1 teaspoon dried basil

½ teaspoon salt

1 tablespoon tomato paste

1 (28-ounce) can tomatoes, chopped

1 cup chicken stock

2 cups elbow macaroni

½ cup heavy cream

salt and freshly ground black pepper

grated Parmesan cheese

1. Pre-heat the pressure cooker using the BROWN setting.

2. Add the butter, onion, celery, garlic, basil and salt and sauté until the vegetables start to soften – about 5 minutes. Add the tomato paste and continue to cook for another 2 to 3 minutes.

3. Add tomatoes, chicken stock and dried pasta. Stir and lock the lid in place.

4. Pressure cook on HIGH for 5 minutes.

5. Release the pressure using the QUICK-RELEASE method and carefully remove the lid. Stir in the heavy cream and season to taste with salt and pepper. Let the pasta sit in the cooker for about 5 minutes or until it is cool enough to eat. Serve with the grated Parmesan cheese sprinkled on top.

Try using half-and-half or milk in this recipe instead of the heavy cream for a lighter meal.

Farfalle Putanesca

Putanesca generally refers to a pasta sauce made with southern Italian ingredients such as capers, olives, garlic and often anchovies. I love anchovies, but you don't have to be an anchovy-lover in order to like this dish. They give a nice salty note to the sauce, but shouldn't overpower it. They are like the secret ingredient!

Serves
4

Cooking Time
8 Minutes

Release Method
Quick-release

1 tablespoon olive oil

4 fillets anchovies, chopped
(or 2 teaspoons anchovy paste)

1 clove garlic, minced

2 tablespoons capers, rinsed

¾ cup pitted black olives, halved

1 (28-ounce) can tomatoes, chopped

2 tablespoons tomato paste

½ pound farfalle or bowtie pasta
(about 4 cups)

1 cup water

freshly ground black pepper

¼ cup chopped fresh parsley

grated Parmesan cheese (optional)

1. Pre-heat the pressure cooker using the BROWN setting.

2. Add the oil and sauté the anchovies and garlic for a minute or two, until the anchovies start to melt. Add the capers, black olives, tomatoes and tomato paste and bring to a simmer. Add the pasta and water and stir well. Season with freshly ground black pepper and lock the lid in place.

3. Pressure cook on HIGH for 8 minutes.

4. Release the pressure using the QUICK-RELEASE method and then let the pasta sit with the lid on for 5 minutes. It needs this time to cool to an edible temperature and finish cooking the pasta. Carefully remove the lid. Stir well and add the parsley. Season to taste with salt (you shouldn't need much if any) and freshly ground black pepper, and serve with grated Parmesan cheese if desired.

Tinned anchovies are good in your cupboard for up to a year. Once you open them and have leftovers, store them in an airtight container and refrigerate. They will hold that way for about two months. Remember, you can use just a little anchovy as a seasoning for so many things – from pasta sauces to dips, to salad dressings and stews.

Spinach Cheese Ravioli
with Zucchini and Marinara

This dish is really two recipes in one! You can stop after you make the marinara and use that as a sauce for any pasta, or you can keep going and add the zucchini and ravioli for a delicious and simple meal.

Serves
6

Cooking Time
5 + 4 Minutes

Release Method
Quick-release

3 tablespoons olive oil

3 cloves garlic, finely chopped

pinch crushed red pepper flakes

1 teaspoon dried oregano

1 (28-ounce) can tomatoes, chopped

1 (28-ounce) can crushed tomatoes

½ cup water

1 teaspoon salt, plus more for seasoning

3 zucchini, sliced ¼-inch thick

1 pound (about 45) small frozen spinach and cheese raviolis

½ cup water

½ cup fresh basil leaves, shredded

grated Parmesan cheese

1. Place the olive oil, garlic and pepper flakes in the pressure cooker and then turn on the BROWN setting. Sauté the garlic and crushed red pepper flakes until the garlic is fragrant, but do not brown.

2. Add the oregano, tomatoes, ½ cup of water and salt, and lock the lid in place.

3. Pressure cook on HIGH for 5 minutes.

4. Release the pressure using the QUICK-RELEASE method and carefully remove the lid. Stir in the zucchini slices and the frozen raviolis, along with another ½ cup of water. Stir well and lock the lid in place.

5. Pressure cook on HIGH for 4 minutes.

6. Release the pressure using the QUICK-RELEASE method and carefully remove the lid. Let the food cool to an edible temperature before sprinkling with the fresh basil and serve with the grated Parmesan cheese.

Substitution

You can substitute any kind of ravioli in this recipe – beef ravioli, mushroom ravioli or just cheese ravioli all work beautifully.

Fusilli with Hot Italian Sausage, Tomatoes, Arugula and Black Olives

The key ingredient in this pasta dish is the Italian sausage, so use the best you can find. Make sure it is raw and not pre-cooked sausage - the fat and spicy flavor from the sausage will come out as the sausage cooks and flavor the rest of the ingredients.

Serves
4

Cooking Time
5 Minutes

Release Method
Quick-release

1 tablespoon olive oil

1 pound (3 to 4 links) raw hot Italian sausage, casings removed and crumbled

1 medium onion, chopped

1 clove garlic, crushed

1 teaspoon salt

1 teaspoon dried oregano

1 (28-ounce) can diced tomatoes

1 cup chicken stock

1 cup pitted black olives, sliced

3 cups fusilli pasta

3 to 4 cups arugula

freshly ground black pepper

1 cup grated Asiago cheese

1. Pre-heat the pressure cooker using the BROWN setting.

2. Add the oil, sausage, onion, garlic, salt and oregano. Cook for 5 to 6 minutes, stirring occasionally. Add the tomatoes, chicken stock, olives and dried pasta. Stir, doing your best to submerge the pasta in the sauce, and lock the lid in place.

3. Pressure cook on HIGH for 5 minutes.

4. Release the pressure using the QUICK-RELEASE method and carefully remove the lid. Stir in the arugula. Return the lid to the cooker and let the pasta sit for a few minutes to cool to an edible temperature. Serve with freshly ground black pepper and grated Asiago cheese.

If you can't find Asiago cheese, try Parmesan or Pecorino Romano cheese.

Pasta Primer

Cooking pasta in the pressure cooker is contrary to all commonly accepted principles of cooking pasta and yet, it works! If you're not a believer that pasta can come out of a pressure cooker cooked al dente with great flavor, don't worry because no one ever believes it at first. The bonus of cooking pasta under pressure is that you can actually cook it in the sauce, giving the pasta extra flavor and completing two jobs at once. Here are some rules and some tips for cooking pasta under pressure:

■ **Use small shaped pasta rather than long noodles like spaghetti, linguine and fettuccine.**

The pasta needs to be covered with liquid in the cooker and long noodles won't fit into most cookers very easily. Penne, macaroni, fusilli, rotini, shells, farfalle or any small shape work well.

■ **Avoid nesting shapes of pasta, like orecchiette.**

They have a tendency to nest inside each other making it take twice as long to cook and will come out of the cooker undercooked and stuck together.

■ **Remember that the pasta will absorb liquid during the cooking process.**

That's good because it can help deliver a thicker sauce, but it does need some extra liquid in order to cook. It's good to estimate a 2:1 ratio by volume of pasta to liquid in a recipe.

■ **The liquid in a pasta recipe doesn't need to be water.**

Using stock or wine or the liquid from a can of tomatoes can make for very tasty pasta.

■ **To figure out how long to cook pasta in the pressure cooker, simply cut the cooking time from the package of pasta in half.**

For example, a 12-minute traditional pasta cooking time will become 6 minutes in the pressure cooker.

■ **Use the QUICK-RELEASE method of releasing the pressure for pasta to stop the cooking process.**

Even after the pressure has been released and the lid is off the cooker, the pasta will continue to absorb liquid and cook, but you will need to let the pasta cool to an edible temperature regardless. That waiting time is perfect for melting cheese on top if you're so inclined.

■ **Never fill the cooker more than half full.**

You should never fill a pressure cooker more than two thirds full at any time and since pasta expands as it cooks, you need to leave extra room.

■ **If you're cooking pasta on its own in the pressure cooker, add some oil to the pot.**

This will help control any foaming of the pasta as it cooks, which could interfere with a pressure valve.

Chili Macaroni

Everyone loves a chili mac – the classic combination of chili and macaroni and cheese. Making it in the pressure cooker means that you can love it sooner – in just 5 minutes!

Serves
4 to 6

Cooking Time
5 Minutes

Release Method
Quick-release

1 tablespoon vegetable oil

1 pound lean ground beef

1 onion, finely chopped

2 cloves garlic, minced

1 red bell pepper, chopped

1 yellow bell pepper, chopped

1 Jalapeño pepper, sliced with or without the seeds (optional)

3 tablespoons chili powder

¼ teaspoon cayenne pepper

1 teaspoon salt

1 (28-ounce) can tomatoes, chopped

1 cup beef stock

1 (15-ounce) can kidney beans, drained and rinsed

½ pound elbow macaroni

salt and freshly ground black pepper

2 cups grated Pepperjack or Cheddar cheese

sour cream for garnish (optional)

1. Pre-heat the pressure cooker using the BROWN setting.

2. Add the oil and brown the beef, breaking it up as you do. Add the onion, garlic, bell peppers, Jalapeño pepper, chili powder, cayenne pepper and salt and cook for just a couple minutes more. Stir in the tomatoes, beef stock, beans and macaroni, and lock the lid in place.

3. Pressure cook on HIGH for 5 minutes.

4. Release the pressure using the QUICK-RELEASE method and carefully remove the lid. Give the ingredients a good stir and season to taste with more salt and freshly ground black pepper. Stir in the grated cheese and serve with a dollop of sour cream if you like.

Did You Know...?

You can use dried beans for this recipe instead of the canned kidney beans. Cook ½ cup of dried kidney beans, covered with water, at HIGH pressure in the cooker for 6 minutes. Let the pressure release NATURALLY. Then drain and proceed with the recipe as written.

Turkey Tetrazzini

Turkey Tetrazzini used to be something I really only had after Thanksgiving, using up any left-over turkey. It doesn't have to be a once-a-year meal, however. You can make it in five minutes in the pressure cooker using ground turkey instead of leftover turkey pieces and it's just as delicious.

Serves
4

Cooking Time
5 Minutes

Release Method
Quick-release

1 tablespoon olive oil

1 pound ground turkey, or leftover turkey pieces

1 onion, chopped

3 ribs celery, chopped

8 ounces button mushrooms, sliced

1 teaspoon dried thyme

1 teaspoon salt

freshly ground black pepper, to taste

¼ cup dry sherry

2 cups chicken stock

3 cups egg noodles (about 5 ounces)

⅔ cup heavy cream

1 cup frozen peas, thawed

½ cup grated Parmesan cheese, plus more for garnish

¼ cup chopped fresh parsley

1 to 2 tablespoons finely chopped lemon zest (optional)

1. Pre-heat the pressure cooker using the BROWN setting.

2. Add the olive oil and brown the ground turkey for a few minutes, breaking it up with a spoon or spatula. Add the onion, celery, mushrooms, thyme, salt and pepper to the pressure cooker and cook for another 5 minutes, or until the vegetables start to soften. Add the sherry, chicken stock and egg noodles and stir. Try to push the egg noodles below the level of liquid and lock the lid in place.

3. Pressure cook on HIGH for 5 minutes.

4. Release the pressure using the QUICK-RELEASE method and carefully remove the lid. Turn the pressure cooker to the BROWN setting and add the cream and peas. Simmer for a couple of minutes, turn off the heat and add the Parmesan cheese and parsley. Stir well, season to taste with salt and freshly ground black pepper and serve with the lemon zest and more Parmesan cheese sprinkled on top.

Substitution

Sherry is a Spanish fortified wine made from white grapes. It comes in a variety of styles and for this recipe (and most savory cooking purposes) you want to use the driest variety, called Fino Sherry. If you don't have any sherry on hand, use a dry white wine.

Lamb Bolognese with Pistachio Gremolata

Gremolata is the name of a very simple herb topping made of lemon zest, parsley and garlic. Here, I've replaced the garlic with pistachios, and it adds a nice zing and crunch to the final dish. It dresses up a Bolognese in just the right way.

Serves
6

Cooking Time
15 Minutes

Release Method
Quick-release

½ pound lean ground beef

1 pound ground lamb

2 tablespoons olive oil

1 onion, finely chopped

2 carrots, finely chopped

2 ribs celery, finely chopped

2 cloves garlic, minced

salt and freshly ground black pepper

4 sprigs fresh thyme

1 teaspoon ground cinnamon

1 bay leaf

1 teaspoon dried oregano

½ cup red wine

½ cup beef stock

1 (28-ounce) can diced tomatoes

3 tablespoons tomato paste

1 cup grated Parmesan cheese
(plus more for garnish if desired)

For the Gremolata:

½ cup shelled unsalted pistachios, toasted

2 tablespoons finely chopped lemon zest

2 tablespoons finely chopped fresh parsley

½ teaspoon salt

1. Pre-heat the pressure cooker using the BROWN setting.

2. Brown the ground lamb and beef in batches. Remove the browned meat with a slotted spoon and set aside. Drain away and discard of the fat between batches.

3. Add the olive oil to the cooker and sauté the onion, carrots, celery and garlic together until tender and lightly browned – about 10 minutes. Add the salt, pepper, thyme, cinnamon, bay leaf and oregano and cook for another minute. Pour in the wine and stir, scraping the bottom of the cooker to incorporate any bits of flavor from the pan into the sauce. Let the mixture simmer for a minute. Add the beef stock, tomatoes and tomato paste. Return the meat to the cooker, stir and lock the lid in place.

4. Pressure cook on HIGH for 15 minutes.

5. While the Bolognese is cooking, make the gremolata. Process the pistachio nuts in a food processor until finely chopped, or chop finely with a knife. Combine the nuts with the lemon zest, parsley and salt in a small bowl and set aside.

6. Release the pressure using the QUICK-RELEASE method and carefully remove the lid. Let the sauce sit for 5 to 10 minutes to come to an edible temperature. Remove the thyme sprigs and discard. Season to taste with salt and freshly ground black pepper and stir the Parmesan cheese into the sauce until it melts. When ready to serve, ladle the Bolognese over cooked pasta (this is especially nice over pappardelle noodles) and top with the pistachio gremolata and some more grated Parmesan cheese.

Substitution

Not a fan of lamb? This is nice with all beef too!

Penne Carbonara

Pasta Carbonara is like having breakfast for dinner, but better! Eggs, bacon and cheese tossed together quickly while the pasta is piping hot makes for a great dinner any night of the week.

Serves
4 to 6

Cooking Time
6 Minutes

Release Method
Quick-release

8 ounces bacon (about 6 strips)

1 clove garlic, smashed

1 pound penne pasta

3 eggs, lightly beaten

1¼ cups finely grated Pecorino Romano cheese (about 1 ounce)

1¼ cups finely grated Parmigiano-Reggiano cheese (about 1 ounce)

½ cup chopped fresh parsley

lots of freshly ground black pepper

1. Pre-heat the pressure cooker using the BROWN setting.

2. Add the bacon and garlic clove and cook until the fat has been rendered out and the bacon is crispy – about 6 to 8 minutes. Remove the bacon with a slotted spoon, transfer to a paper-towel lined plate and set aside. Drain off the fat from the cooker and discard.

3. Add the pasta to the cooker, along with 4 cups of water and lock the lid in place.

4. Pressure cook on HIGH for 6 minutes.

5. While the pasta is cooking, beat the eggs with the cheeses in a bowl.

6. Release the pressure using the QUICK-RELEASE method and carefully remove the lid. Reserve half a cup of the pasta water. Drain the pasta and immediately return the pasta to the hot cooker. Stirring constantly, pour the egg and cheese mixture into the pasta and return the bacon to the cooker. Stir well and add the parsley and the freshly ground black pepper. Use the residual pasta water to thin the pasta if needed. Serve immediately.

Try tossing some halved cherry tomatoes and fresh basil, arugula or spinach into this pasta at the last minute for a nice colorful variation on the classic.

Roasted Red Pepper Rigatoni with Feta Cheese

Here's another super easy pasta recipe that can be made in less than ten minutes using dried pasta. You can definitely substitute an onion for the leek here, but the leek does add a nice gentle note to the dish, along with a touch of color.

Serves
4 to 6

Cooking Time
7 Minutes

Release Method
Quick-release

1 tablespoon olive oil

1 leek, chopped

1 clove garlic, sliced

1 teaspoon dried basil

1 teaspoon salt

1 (15.5-ounce) jar roasted red peppers (about 5 whole roasted peppers), sliced

3 fresh tomatoes, chopped

3 cups chicken stock

12 ounces rigatoni pasta (about 5 cups)

freshly ground black pepper

½ cup cream

1 cup crumbled feta cheese

¼ cup chopped fresh parsley or basil

1. Pre-heat the pressure cooker using the BROWN setting.

2. Add the olive oil and sauté the leek, garlic, basil, and salt for 2 to 3 minutes. Add the roasted red peppers, tomatoes, stock and dried pasta. Season with freshly ground black pepper and stir everything together. Lock the lid in place.

3. Pressure cook on HIGH for 7 minutes.

4. Release the pressure using the QUICK-RELEASE method and carefully remove the lid. Stir in the cream and feta cheese and let the pasta cool to an edible temperature for a couple of minutes. Garnish with fresh parsley or basil and enjoy!

Did You Know...?

Leeks are the elegant, mild-flavored member of the onion family. They can be dirty, however, getting soil caught between their leaves as they push up out of the ground. Make sure you clean them well by cutting off the dark green top of the leek where it naturally wants to break if you bend the leek from end to end. Then, slice the leek in half lengthwise and soak it in cold water for 10 minutes or so, separating the leaves with your hands to remove any embedded dirt. Dry the leeks with a paper towel gently before using.

Turkey Bolognese Rigatoni

Using ground turkey instead of beef, and adding just a hint of anise flavor with the fennel seed, makes this Bolognese a little different from the traditional pasta sauce. What's really special, however, is the fact that the dried pasta gets thrown into the pressure cooker at the same time making it the fastest Bolognese in... well, ever!

Serves
4

Cooking Time
8 Minutes

Release Method
Quick-release

1 tablespoon olive oil

2 pounds ground turkey

1 onion, finely chopped

2 cloves garlic, minced

2 ribs celery, finely chopped

1 teaspoon dried basil

1 teaspoon fennel seed

½ cup white wine

1 (28-ounce) can crushed tomatoes

2 tablespoons tomato paste

2 cups chicken stock

2 teaspoons salt

freshly ground black pepper

12 ounces rigatoni pasta (¾ of a box)

¼ cup chopped fresh parsley

½ cup grated Parmigiano-Reggiano cheese

1. Pre-heat the pressure cooker using the BROWN setting.

2. Add the oil and brown the ground turkey in batches until cooked through. Transfer the turkey to a bowl using a slotted spoon, and pour off all but one tablespoon of the fat from the cooker.

3. Add the onion, garlic and celery to the cooker and sauté until the onion starts to become tender – about 5 minutes. Stir in the dried basil and fennel seed and cook for another minute or so. Stir in the white wine, tomatoes, tomato paste, chicken stock, salt and pepper. Return the meat to the cooker, stir in the rigatoni, pushing the pasta below the level of the liquid, and lock the lid in place.

4. Pressure cook on HIGH for 8 minutes.

5. Release the pressure using the QUICK-RELEASE method and carefully remove the lid. Let the pasta cool to an edible temperature – about 5 minutes. Stir in the parsley and season to taste with salt and freshly ground black pepper. Serve with grated Parmesan cheese at the table.

BLUE JEAN Chef *Lighten Up*

I like to use either all ground turkey thighs or a mix of ground turkey breasts and thighs for this recipe because the thighs have a more robust flavor, but you can use just breast meat if you want to make this recipe a little lighter.

Cavatappi con Vongole
(Pasta with Clams)

When I was a little girl, my mother used to make spaghetti con vongole and it was one of my favorite pastas. I liked the way it tasted and I LOVED just saying the name! Here's a version using fresh clams and curly cavatappi pasta.

Serves
4

Cooking Time
4 Minutes

Release Method
Quick-release

4 pounds (about 50) fresh littleneck or Manila clams

2 tablespoons olive oil

2 cloves garlic, sliced

⅛ to ¼ teaspoon crushed red pepper flakes

1 cup white wine

1 cup chicken stock

8 ounces cavatappi pasta (about 2 heaping cups)

2 cups halved cherry tomatoes

½ cup coarse or panko breadcrumbs

4 tablespoons butter, divided

½ lemon, zest and juice

salt and freshly ground black pepper

½ cup chopped fresh parsley

extra virgin olive oil

1. Before you start cooking or prepping, soak the clams in tap water (room temperature). Let them soak while you prepare the rest of the recipe, or for at least 30 minutes. They will spit out sand. Then, pick the clams out of the water and give the shells a scrub under running water to remove any barnacles or dirt. Discard any clams that are open or have cracked shells.

2. Add the olive oil, garlic and crushed red pepper flakes to the pressure cooker and then pre-heat the pressure cooker using the BROWN setting. Just before the garlic starts to turn brown on the edges, add the wine and stock. Stir in the pasta and tomatoes, and add the clams on top. Lock the lid in place.

3. Pressure cook on HIGH for 4 minutes.

4. While the pasta is cooking, toast the breadcrumbs in 2 table-spoons of butter using a small skillet over medium heat. Set aside when nicely browned and crunchy.

5. Release the pressure using the QUICK-RELEASE method and carefully remove the lid. Remove the clams to a serving bowl with a big slotted spoon, discarding any clams that did not fully open. Add the remaining butter and lemon juice to the pot and season the broth to taste with salt and freshly ground black pepper. Toss the clams and pasta together and pour the broth over the top. Sprinkle the chopped parsley, lemon zest and toasted breadcrumbs on top, drizzle with olive oil and don't forget to put a bowl on the table for everyone's clamshells!

 Substitution

Yes, traditionally pasta con vongole is made with spaghetti. However, you can't cook long pasta like spaghetti in a pressure cooker, so this recipe uses a small-shaped pasta. If you can't find cavatappi in your grocery store, choose another shape of pasta with an 8-minute cooking time.

Sunday Gravy

Being Canadian, calling a tomato sauce "Gravy" was very foreign to me, but thirteen years living in eastern Pennsylvania has made it very familiar. In this part of the country "Gravy" denotes a tomato sauce that has meat cooked in it and is an Italian-American tradition on a Sunday. I turned to one of my favorite Northeastern American Italian friends for her expertise on this recipe–thanks, Lisa! In typical Italian fashion, this makes a huge amount of food, so be sure you use a big pressure cooker.

Serves
6 to 8

Cooking Time
20 Minutes

Release Method
Natural

Meatballs:
1 pound lean ground beef
½ cup diced onion
¾ cup panko breadcrumbs
¾ cup grated Parmesan cheese
1 teaspoon salt
⅛ teaspoon pepper
½ teaspoon dried oregano
1 tablespoon dried parsley
½ teaspoon Worcestershire sauce
1 egg, lightly beaten

Sauce:
1 pound sweet Italian sausage
1½ pounds pork neck bones
(or country style ribs)
1 onion, finely chopped
1 green pepper, finely chopped
2 cloves garlic, minced
2 tablespoons Italian seasoning
1 teaspoon dried oregano
1 tablespoon sugar
1 teaspoon salt
freshly ground black pepper
1 cup red wine
1 cup beef stock
1 (28-ounce) can crushed tomatoes
1 (28-ounce) can petite diced tomatoes
3 tablespoons tomato paste
½ cup grated Parmesan cheese
¼ cup chopped fresh parsley

1. Start by making the meatballs. Combine the first ten ingredients in a bowl and roll into 12 evenly sized meatballs. If desired, brown these meatballs on a sheet pan in the oven at 400º F for 20 minutes while you prepare the rest of the ingredients. Otherwise, set the meatballs aside.

2. Pre-heat the pressure cooker using the BROWN setting.

3. Brown the Italian sausage and pork bones on all sides. Set the meat aside and pour off all but one tablespoon of the fat. Add the onion, green pepper and garlic to the cooker and cook until the onion starts to become soft – about 5 minutes. Stir in the Italian seasoning, oregano, sugar, salt and pepper and cook for another minute or so. Add the red wine, beef stock, crushed and diced tomatoes, and tomato paste, and return all the browned meat and meatballs to the cooker. Stir gently and lock the lid in place.

4. Pressure cook on HIGH for 20 minutes.

5. Let the pressure drop NATURALLY and carefully remove the lid. Transfer the meat from the sauce to a serving dish. Stir the grated Parmesan cheese and fresh parsley into the sauce and season to taste with salt and pepper. Transfer the sauce to a separate serving vessel. Serve the meat and sauce with your favorite pasta and some extra Parmesan cheese at the table.

Take Sunday Gravy one step further and serve ricotta cheese alongside the Parmesan cheese at the table. The plate is really over the top and delicious with a dollop of ricotta!

Poultry

Chicken and Lemon-Chive Dumplings

Greek Chicken and Potatoes

Chicken Marsala Stew with Mushrooms, Peas and Potatoes

Honey Mustard Chicken with Orange and Rosemary Potatoes

Salsa Chicken Thighs with Rice

Lemon Oregano Chicken Breasts with Orzo, Olives and Feta Cheese

Chicken Pot Pie with Leeks and Lemon

Chicken Tikka Masala

Turkey Breast with Spinach, Feta, Lemon and Walnut Stuufing

Turkey Breast with Italian Sausage and Dried Cherry Stuffing

BBQ Turkey Mushroom Meatloaf

Chicken and Lemon-Chive Dumplings

Chicken and Dumplings just screams comfort food no matter which type of dumpling is involved – the flat rolled dumpling, or the fluffy dropped dumpling. I prefer the dropped dumpling, probably because that's what my mother made when I was a child. Adding the lemon zest and chives to the dumpling batter lightens and brightens the dumplings just a little. The dumplings actually cook on top of the piping hot chicken stew at the very end of cooking.

Serves
6

Cooking Time
10 Minutes

Release Method
Quick-release

2 tablespoons olive oil

1 onion, chopped

2 ribs celery, chopped

3 carrots, chopped

2 cloves garlic, smashed

1 teaspoon dried thyme

½ teaspoon dried rosemary

½ cup white wine or dry vermouth

4 cups good quality chicken stock

3 cups diced red-skinned potatoes (about 1 pound)

2 pounds boneless skinless chicken breasts and thighs, cut into bite-sized pieces

2 teaspoons salt

freshly ground black pepper

1½ cups Bisquick® mix

½ cup milk

6 tablespoons chopped fresh chives

2 tablespoons lemon zest (about 2 lemons)

¼ cup butter, softened at room temperature

½ cup flour

¼ cup heavy cream

¼ chopped fresh parsley

1. Pre-heat the pressure cooker using the BROWN setting.

2. Add the olive oil to the cooker and sauté the onion, celery and carrots until they start to become tender – about 5 minutes. Add the garlic and dried spices and cook for another 2 minutes. Add the white wine (or vermouth), chicken stock, potatoes and chicken pieces. Season with salt and freshly ground black pepper, give everything a good stir and lock the lid in place.

3. Pressure cook on HIGH for 10 minutes.

4. While the stew is cooking, make your dumplings. Combine the Bisquick® mix with the milk, chives and lemon zest in a bowl and stir until the dough forms. Set aside.

5. In a second bowl, combine the butter and flour to form a paste (called a beurre manié) and set aside.

6. Release the pressure using the QUICK-RELEASE method and carefully remove the lid. Ladle some of the hot liquid from the cooker into the bowl with the beurre manié and whisk well. Pour the mixture back into the cooker, and add the cream and parsley. Return the cooker to the BROWN setting and bring everything to a gentle simmer. Season to taste with salt and freshly ground black pepper.

7. Drop the dumplings by the large spoonful onto the surface of the stew. Then, put the lid on the cooker, turn it off and let the chicken and dumplings sit for at least 10 minutes before serving.

Substitution

If you don't want to open a whole bottle of wine for a recipe, substituting vermouth is a good idea. An open bottle of vermouth keeps for about three months when stored in the refrigerator. Substitute dry vermouth for white wine, and sweet vermouth for red wine.

Greek Chicken and Potatoes

We don't generally put cinnamon in many savory dishes in American or Canadian cuisine, but it's a common occurrence in Greek foods. I think it adds a lot of interest to a dish, even when you add just a small amount as in the recipe below.

Serves
4

Cooking Time
8 Minutes

Release Method
Quick-release

1 tablespoon olive oil

4 boneless, skinless chicken breasts, each cut into two chunks

salt and freshly ground black pepper

1 onion, chopped

1 clove garlic, sliced

2 red bell peppers, julienned

1 teaspoon dried oregano

1 bay leaf

1 teaspoon salt

2 tablespoons tomato paste

¼ teaspoon ground cinnamon

½ cup white wine

1½ cups chicken stock

1 (14-ounce) can crushed tomatoes

4 russet potatoes, peeled and cut into 1-inch wide wedges

1 cup crumbled feta cheese

¼ cup chopped fresh parsley

1. Pre-heat the pressure cooker using the BROWN setting.

2. Add the olive oil to the cooker. Season the chicken with salt and pepper and brown for about 2 minutes per side. Remove the chicken and set aside.

3. Add the onion, garlic, red pepper and oregano to the cooker and cook for 3 to 4 minutes. Add the bay leaf, salt, tomato paste and cinnamon and cook for 2 more minutes. Add the white wine and bring to a simmer for a couple of minutes. Add the chicken stock, tomatoes and potatoes to the cooker and stir. Return the chicken to the pot and lock the lid in place.

4. Pressure cook on HIGH for 8 minutes.

5. Release the pressure using the QUICK-RELEASE method and carefully remove the lid. Let the chicken cool to an edible temperature and serve with feta cheese and parsley sprinkled on top.

In a rush? You can skip the browning step in the recipe and just put the un-browned chicken into the cooker in step 4 instead. It may not be as attractive, but it will be covered with tomato sauce and you can always just turn the lights down low. 😊

Chicken Marsala Stew
with Mushrooms, Peas and Potatoes

This recipe takes all the flavors of Chicken Marsala and puts them into a stew. I like to use hearty, flavorful mushrooms, like Crimini or Baby Bella mushrooms for this dish, but you can use button mushrooms if that's what you have on hand.

Serves
4

Cooking Time
6 Minutes

Release Method
Quick-release

½ cup all-purpose flour

1 teaspoon salt

freshly ground black pepper

4 boneless skinless chicken breasts, cut into 2-inch chunks (about 2 pounds)

1 tablespoon olive oil

1 onion, finely chopped

2 carrots, sliced into ¼-inch rounds

2 cloves garlic, minced

12 ounces Crimini or Baby Bella mushrooms, sliced

1 pound white potatoes, cut into bite-sized chunks

½ teaspoon dried sage

¾ cup dry Marsala wine

2 cups chicken stock

1 cup frozen peas, thawed

¼ cup chopped fresh parsley

½ cup heavy cream

1. Pre-heat the pressure cooker using the BROWN setting.

2. Combine the flour, salt, and a few grinds of freshly ground black pepper in a bowl. Toss the chicken pieces in the flour, shaking off the excess.

3. Add olive oil to the cooker and brown the chicken well on all sides in batches, removing the browned chicken to a side plate. Add the onion, carrots, garlic and mushrooms to the cooker and sauté until the onion just starts to become tender – about 5 minutes. Add the potatoes and sage and cook for another minute. Return the browned chicken pieces to the cooker and stir well. Pour in the Marsala wine and chicken stock, and lock the lid in place.

4. Pressure cook on HIGH for 6 minutes.

5. Release the pressure using the QUICK-RELEASE method and carefully remove the lid. Stir in the peas, parsley and heavy cream and season to taste with salt and freshly ground black pepper. Serve over rice or noodles.

BLUE JEAN Chef Did You Know...?

Marsala is a fortified wine that originated in the Sicilian town of Marsala. Marsala wines are classified into several categories by color and sweetness, but at a very basic level you'll just need to choose between sweet or dry Marsala when you do your shopping for this recipe. Though you can use a sweet marsala for this dish, it changes the final flavor quite dramatically. It is generally agreed upon that a classic Chicken Marsala calls for the dry variety.

Honey Mustard Chicken with Orange and Rosemary Potatoes

Who doesn't love the combination of honey and mustard? When you combine it with orange and rosemary flavors, it just gets even better! Use a good, hearty whole-grain mustard – it gives a more interesting look to the chicken at the end.

Serves
4

Cooking Time
6 Minutes

Release Method
Quick-release

1 tablespoon olive oil

4 pounds skinless chicken breasts and thighs, bones left in

salt and freshly ground black pepper

1 white onion, sliced

2 sprigs fresh rosemary

16 to 20 fingerling or small white potatoes, left whole

1 cup chicken stock

½ cup fresh orange juice
(about two oranges)

¼ cup whole grain mustard

¼ cup honey

1 tablespoon finely chopped orange zest

1 tablespoon finely chopped fresh rosemary

1 tablespoon butter (optional)

1. Pre-heat the pressure cooker using the BROWN setting.

2. Add the olive oil, season the chicken with salt and freshly ground black pepper and sear the chicken on all sides until nicely browned. Remove the chicken from the cooker and set aside. Add the onion and rosemary sprigs and sauté until the onion starts to become tender – about 5 minutes. Add the potatoes and stir well to coat everything with the oil. Season with salt and pour in the chicken stock and orange juice. Return the chicken to the cooker. Combine the mustard, honey and orange zest in a small bowl and pour the mixture over the chicken pieces. Lock the lid in place.

3. Pressure cook on HIGH for 6 minutes.

4. Release the pressure using the QUICK-RELEASE method and carefully remove the lid. Let the chicken and potatoes cool slightly before serving, garnishing with chopped fresh rosemary and butter on the potatoes if desired.

Make a sauce for the chicken at the end of cooking, by simmering and reducing the braising liquid left in the cooker while the chicken and potatoes cool on a platter for a little while. When the sauce is thick enough to coat the back of a spoon, pour it over the chicken and garnish with a few fresh rosemary leaves.

Salsa Chicken Thighs with Rice

The flavor and spiciness of this super easy dish depends entirely on the salsa that you use. So buy a salsa that you like and make sure it is the right level of spiciness for you. If you'd like it even spicier, add a sliced Jalapeño pepper to the rice with the bell peppers.

Serves
4

Cooking Time
5 Minutes

Release Method
Quick-release

4 to 6 large skinless chicken thighs

1 teaspoon salt

½ teaspoon chili powder

1 tablespoon olive oil

½ red onion, finely chopped (about ½ cup)

1 red bell pepper, finely diced

1 green bell pepper, finely diced

1 cup basmati rice (basmati is best, but regular long-grain can be substituted)

1 cup chicken stock

¾ cup jarred salsa

½ cup grated Monterey Jack cheese (about 3 ounces)

¼ cup chopped fresh cilantro

1. Pre-heat the pressure cooker using the BROWN setting.

2. Season the chicken thighs with the salt and chili powder. Add the oil to the cooker and sear the thighs on both sides until well browned. Remove the chicken from the cooker and set aside. Add the onion and peppers and sauté until the onion starts to become tender – about 5 minutes. Add the rice and stir well to coat everything with the oil. Season the rice with salt, pour in the chicken stock and return the chicken thighs to the cooker, resting them on top of the rice. Top each chicken thigh with the salsa and lock the lid in place.

3. Pressure cook on HIGH for 5 minutes.

4. Release the pressure using the QUICK-RELEASE method and carefully remove the lid. Sprinkle the cheese on top of the thighs and return the lid to the cooker for another 5 minutes while the chicken rests and cools to an edible temperature. Transfer the chicken thighs and rice to a serving platter and sprinkle the cilantro on top before serving.

Did You Know...?

Cooking chicken with the bone in produces a more flavorful result. In the pressure cooker, skin doesn't have a chance to get crispy, so I tend to use chicken that is skinless, but still on the bone.

Chicken Scoop

The short cooking time for chicken in a pressure cooker really surprises me every time. Depending on how the chicken is prepared (bone-in versus bone-out; thighs versus breast; cut into strips or chunks versus left whole) cooking chicken in the pressure cooker can take as little as one minute, or as much as 35 minutes. Regardless, the cooking time in a pressure cooker is dramatically less than what it would take with traditional cooking methods. Now, contrary to popular belief, you can over-cook and dry out a chicken in the pressure cooker, so it is important to time your recipe. Here are some tips to help you prepare moist, delicious chicken dishes.

■ **Bone-in chicken will result in more flavorful chicken.**

This is not news! The bone imparts a great deal of flavor in chicken dishes, so whenever possible, use chicken pieces that are on the bone.

■ **It's better to remove the skin.**

Unfortunately, the skin never has a chance to crisp in a pressure cooker. Even when you brown the chicken pieces first, the skin tends to get soggy and unappetizing after pressure-cooking. It also contributes to the fat content in the recipe, which often results in a layer of grease on top of the food. I've found it best to remove the skin, but leave the bone in.

■ **Browning first makes a difference.**

Even without the skin, it's good to give the chicken pieces (or any meat for that matter) some color before pressure-cooking. You'll add to the flavor of the chicken this way, and you'll also make it more attractive and appealing at the same time.

■ **Natural OR Quick-release.**

You'll find the recipes in this chapter use both natural and quick-release methods to release the pressure from the cooker. There's no rule of thumb when it comes to chicken. In general, all meats benefit from a natural release, but if you want to stop the cooking time in order not to over-cook, you have to use the quick-release method. Sometimes a natural release is actually part of the cooking time of the recipe, so just know that the release methods used in these recipes are intentional and have a direct affect on the tenderness and moisture of the finished chicken.

■ **Cooking from frozen.**

I never recommend cooking anything from a frozen state, but sometimes our busy lives can get the better of us, and planning falls by the wayside. If that should happen to you, you can cook foods that are no more than 1-inch thick from a frozen state. You'll just need to increase the cooking time to compensate.

Lemon Oregano Chicken Breasts with Orzo, Olives and Feta Cheese

Here's a meal that you can serve warm or at room temperature, making it a great meal to take to someone's house or on an outing. It's also great the next day as leftovers!

Serves
4

Cooking Time
4 Minutes

Release Method
Combo

1 lemon, zest and juice

2 teaspoons dried oregano

1 teaspoon salt

freshly ground black pepper

4 boneless, skinless chicken breasts

1 to 2 tablespoons olive oil

½ onion, finely chopped (about ½ cup)

2 carrots, finely chopped

1 clove garlic, smashed

2 cups orzo

1 cup chicken stock

1 cup water

½ cup crumbled feta cheese

¼ cup chopped black olives
(like Kalamata)

1 cup halved cherry tomatoes

¼ cup chopped fresh herbs
(parsley, chives and oregano)

1. Combine the lemon zest, oregano, salt and pepper and sprinkle this mixture over all the chicken breasts.

2. Pre-heat the pressure cooker using the BROWN setting.

3. Add the oil to the cooker and brown the chicken breasts on both sides. Remove the chicken to a plate and set aside. Add the onion, carrots and garlic to the cooker and sauté until the onion starts to become tender – about 5 minutes. Add the orzo, chicken stock and water, and stir. Season with salt and freshly ground black pepper. Return the chicken breasts to the cooker, resting them on top of the orzo and lock the lid in place.

4. Pressure cook on HIGH for 4 minutes.

5. Let the pressure drop NATURALLY for 10 minutes. Then, release any residual pressure using the QUICK-RELEASE method and carefully remove the lid. Remove the chicken breasts to a cutting board to rest. Add the feta cheese, olives, tomatoes and fresh herbs to the orzo and toss. Season the orzo with a squeeze of lemon juice, salt and pepper. Serve the chicken sliced on the bias with the orzo and a fresh green salad.

Orzo is small pasta, shaped like a large grain of rice. The name is derived from Italian for "barley".

Chicken Pot Pie
with Leeks and Lemon

The filling for this pot pie is made so quickly in the pressure cooker that you'd better turn on the oven to bake the puff pastry tops right away! You can buy puff pastry in the freezer section of the grocery store – just remember that you'll have to defrost it overnight in the refrigerator, so plan ahead.

Serves
6

Cooking Time
6 Minutes

Release Method
Quick-release

1 tablespoon olive oil

3 large leeks, cleaned, light green and white part sliced (½-inch slices; about 6 cups)

3 carrots, sliced (¼-inch slices)

3 ribs celery, sliced (¼-inch slices)

6 sprigs fresh thyme

2 cloves garlic, smashed

4 cups chicken stock

2 pounds boneless skinless chicken breasts, cut into bite-sized pieces

½ teaspoon salt

freshly ground black pepper

1 sheet puff pastry

1 egg, lightly beaten

¼ cup butter

5 tablespoons flour

¼ cup heavy cream

1 tablespoon lemon zest

1 cup frozen peas, defrosted

¼ cup chopped fresh parsley

¼ cup chopped fresh tarragon or chives

1. Pre-heat the pressure cooker using the BROWN setting and pre-heat the oven to 400° F.

2. Add the olive oil and sauté the leeks, carrots, celery, thyme and garlic until the leeks soften – about 6 to 8 minutes. Pour in the chicken stock and add the chicken pieces. Season with salt and pepper and lock the lid in place.

3. Pressure cooker on HIGH for 6 minutes.

4. While the chicken is cooking, prepare the puff pastry tops. Cut the puff pastry sheet into rounds or squares to suit the size of your serving dish and place on a cookie sheet. Brush the pastry with the beaten egg and transfer the cookie sheet to the 400° F oven for 10 to 12 minutes.

5. Make a roux to thicken the stew by melting butter in a small saucepan over medium heat. Add the flour and whisk together, cooking for about 2 minutes. Set aside.

6. Release the pressure using the QUICK-RELEASE method and carefully remove the lid. Whisk the roux into the stew and bring the mixture to a simmer to thicken. Turn the cooker off, stir in the cream, lemon zest, peas and fresh herbs and let the mixture cool slightly before serving. Serve the chicken stew in a bowl with a round or square of puff pastry on top.

 Shortcut

You can top this dish with a pre-baked biscuit or a pre-baked puff pastry top. That way, you don't have to turn on your oven. Of course, you can also eat this without a top at all, and just enjoy the stew – Chicken à la King!

Chicken Tikka Masala

Though it didn't actually originate in India, Chicken Tikka Masala is a classic Indian take out dinner. It is said to be of British origin, but it has become one of the most popular items ordered at Indian restaurants worldwide. Chunks of chicken are marinated in yogurt and then cooked in a spicy sauce. It's one of my favorites, no matter where it originated!

Serves
4 to 6

Cooking Time
3 Minutes

Release Method
Natural

½ cup plain yogurt (regular or low-fat, but not Greek yogurt)

1 tablespoon ground coriander

2 teaspoons ground cumin

2 teaspoons garam masala

1 tablespoon turmeric

1 teaspoon smoked paprika

pinch of cayenne pepper
(according to taste)

2 teaspoons salt

2 pounds boneless, skinless chicken breasts or thighs, cut into 2-inch strips

2 tablespoons butter

1 onion, finely chopped

2 cloves garlic, minced

1 tablespoon grated fresh ginger

1 (28-ounce) can tomatoes, chopped

2 tablespoons tomato paste

½ cup heavy cream

½ cup water

cilantro leaves, for garnish

1. Combine the yogurt, spices and salt in a bowl, add the chicken and marinate for an hour.

2. Pre-heat the pressure cooker using the BROWN setting.

3. Add the butter to the cooker and sauté the onion, garlic and ginger for a few minutes. Add the chicken and the marinade and stir for another 30 to 60 seconds. Add the tomatoes, tomato paste, heavy cream and water and stir well. Lock the lid in place.

4. Pressure cook on HIGH for 3 minutes.

5. Let the pressure drop NATURALLY and carefully remove the lid. Stir in the fresh cilantro leaves and serve over rice.

Did You Know....?

Fresh ginger freezes really well. Grate it first and then freeze it in tablespoon-sized portions. Then, you'll always have some ready when you need it.

Turkey Breast with Spinach, Feta, Lemon and Walnut Stuffing

This recipe takes a little extra work, but the final result can impress any dinner party guest. I love cooking turkey breast in a pressure cooker because it helps to keep the meat juicy and moist. Once you learn the technique, you'll be able to add your own fillings to vary the recipe.

Serves
4 to 6

Cooking Time
20 Minutes

Release Method
Combo

1 (2- to 2½-pound) skinless turkey breast

10 ounces frozen spinach, thawed, and squeezed dry

1 cup crumbled feta cheese

zest of one lemon

1 teaspoon chopped fresh thyme leaves

½ cup chopped toasted walnuts

salt and freshly ground black pepper

1 to 2 tablespoons olive oil

½ onion, cut into four wedges

1 large carrot, cut into 3-inch lengths and halved lengthwise

1 cup chicken stock

½ cup white wine

2 tablespoons flour

1 tablespoon butter, room temperature

1 tablespoon fresh thyme leaves

1. Butterfly the turkey breast by pressing the turkey breast flat on the cutting board with one hand, while slicing into the turkey breast parallel to the cutting board with the other. Slice into the longest side of the turkey breast, but stop before you cut all the way through. You should then be able to open the turkey breast up like a book, making it twice as wide as it was when you started.

2. Combine the spinach, feta cheese, lemon zest, thyme and toasted walnuts in a bowl. Season the turkey with salt and pepper and then spread the mixture across the entire surface of the opened turkey breast, except for 2 inches from the edge of one of the short sides. Roll the turkey breast up, starting from one short side and ending at the short side with the 2 inches of uncovered meat. Tie the turkey breast closed in several places with kitchen twine.

3. Pre-heat the pressure cooker using the BROWN setting.

4. Season the turkey breast with salt and freshly ground black pepper. Add the oil to the pressure cooker and brown the turkey breast on all sides. Set the browned turkey breast aside. Scatter the onion and carrots in the cooker. (These vegetables will act like a rack, keeping the turkey off the bottom of the cooker.) Place the browned turkey breast on top. Pour in the chicken stock and wine, and lock the lid in place.

5. Pressure cook on HIGH for 20 minutes.

6. Let the pressure drop NATURALLY for 15 minutes. Release any residual pressure using the QUICK-RELEASE method and carefully remove the lid. Transfer the turkey breast to a cutting board and let it rest for at least 5 minutes.

7. While the turkey is resting, make a quick sauce. Combine the flour and butter in small bowl until it forms a paste (a beurre manié). Remove and discard the onions and carrots from the braising liquid and return the pressure cooker to the BROWN setting. Whisk the beurre manié mixture into the liquid in the cooker and bring it to a simmer to thicken. Season to taste with salt and freshly ground black pepper and add the fresh thyme leaves. Slice the turkey breast and serve with the sauce poured over the top.

Turkey Breast with Italian Sausage and Dried Cherry Stuffing

This stuffed turkey breast has a flavor reminiscent of Thanksgiving. There are no bread cubes in the recipe, but breadcrumbs instead, which soak up the delicious flavor from the sausage filling – just like my favorite Thanksgiving side dish!

Serves
4 to 6

Cooking Time
25 Minutes

Release Method
Combo

½ cup dried sour cherries

½ cup port wine

1 (2- to 2½-pound) skinless turkey breast

salt and freshly ground black pepper

½ pound Italian sausage, removed from casing and crumbled

2 teaspoons dried sage
(or 2 tablespoons chopped fresh sage)

1 cup coarse breadcrumbs

½ cup chopped toasted pecans

1 to 2 tablespoons olive oil

½ onion, cut into four wedges

1 large carrot, cut into 3-inch lengths and halved lengthwise

1½ cups chicken stock

2 tablespoons flour

1 tablespoon, room temperature butter

2 tablespoons chopped fresh thyme leaves

1. Soak the dried cherries in the port wine while you prepare the turkey breast and the rest of the stuffing.

2. Butterfly the turkey breast by pressing the turkey breast flat on the cutting board with one hand, while slicing into the turkey breast parallel to the cutting board with the other. Slice into the longest side of the turkey breast, but stop before you cut all the way through. You should then be able to open the turkey breast up like a book, making it twice as wide as it was when you started. Season the turkey with salt and freshly ground black pepper.

3. Combine the sausage, sage, breadcrumbs and pecans in a bowl. Drain the cherries, reserving the port, and add them to the sausage mixture. Season with salt and freshly ground black pepper and spread the stuffing onto the open turkey breast, covering the entire surface, except for 2 inches from the edge of one of the short sides. Roll the turkey breast up, starting from one short side and ending at the short side with the 2 inches of uncovered meat. Tie the turkey breast closed in several places with kitchen twine.

4. Pre-heat the pressure cooker using the BROWN setting.

5. Season the turkey breast with salt and freshly ground black pepper. Add the oil to the pressure cooker and brown the turkey breast on all sides. Set the browned turkey breast aside. Scatter the onion and carrots in the cooker. (These vegetables will act like a rack, keeping the turkey off the bottom of the cooker.) Place the browned turkey breast on top. Pour in the chicken stock and reserved port wine, and lock the lid in place.

6. Pressure cook on HIGH for 25 minutes.

7. Let the pressure drop NATURALLY for 15 minutes. Release any residual pressure using the QUICK-RELEASE method and carefully remove the lid. Transfer the turkey breast to a cutting board and let it rest for at least 5 minutes.

8. While the turkey is resting, make a quick sauce. Combine the flour and butter in small bowl until it forms a paste (a beurre manié). Remove and discard the onions and carrots from the braising liquid and return the pressure cooker to the BROWN setting. Whisk the beurre manié into the liquid in the cooker and bring it to a simmer to thicken. Season to taste with salt and freshly ground black pepper and add the thyme leaves. Slice the turkey breast and serve with the sauce poured over the top.

BBQ Turkey Mushroom Meatloaf

When making meatloaf in a pressure cooker, I used to start by hunting around the kitchen for a pan or baking dish that would fit inside my cooker. I've since learned, however, that if you have a rack and some aluminum foil, you can stop hunting for that dish or pan and the meatloaf holds its shape just as well.

Serves
6

Cooking Time
30 Minutes

Release Method
Natural

1 tablespoon vegetable oil

1 onion, finely chopped

2 cloves garlic, minced

2 pounds ground turkey (breast, thigh or a combination of the two)

8 ounces button mushrooms, finely chopped

1 cup fresh breadcrumbs

½ teaspoon dried thyme

½ teaspoon dried sage

1 egg, lightly beaten

1 tablespoon salt

freshly ground black pepper

1 cup chicken or mushroom stock

1 cup BBQ sauce, plus more for glazing at end

1. Pre-heat the pressure cooker using the BROWN setting, or heat a skillet over medium heat. Add the oil and sauté the onion and garlic until it starts to become tender – about 5 minutes. Transfer the vegetables to a bowl. Add the ground turkey, chopped mushrooms, breadcrumbs, thyme, sage, egg, salt and pepper to the bowl and mix everything together (your hands are a great tool for this) until everything is combined.

2. Spread a piece of aluminum foil out on the counter that is about 20 inches long. Fold the foil so that it is about 7 inches wide. Transfer the meatloaf mixture to the middle of this strip of aluminum foil and shape the mixture into an oval or round loaf-like shape that will fit inside your cooker. Place a rack in the pressure cooker and pour the chicken (or mushroom) stock into the bottom. Use the aluminum foil to transfer the meatloaf to the pressure cooker. Pour the BBQ sauce over the top of the meatloaf. Crumple the ends of the foil a little, tuck them inside the cooker and lock the lid in place.

3. Pressure cook on HIGH for 30 minutes.

4. Let the pressure drop NATURALLY and carefully remove the lid. Remove the meatloaf from the cooker using the foil sling, brush with more BBQ sauce if desired and let the meatloaf cool for about 10 minutes before slicing and serving.

Did You Know...?

In this recipe, the mushrooms do more than just add flavor. They also add moisture, releasing it as they cook in the meatloaf. A food processor makes quick work of finely chopping them.

Beef

Beef Brisket with Onion and Mushroom Gravy

Beef Brisket with Dried Plums, Cognac and Cream

Parmesan Meatballs and Marinara

Corned Beef Reuben Casserole

Beef Braciola with Mushrooms

Sweet Vidalia Onion Joes

Turkish Beef and Eggplant Moussaka

Jiggs Dinner

Hunter's Beef Stew

Beef Dip Sandwiches

Stout-Braised Beef Short Ribs

Curried Beef with Cucumber Yogurt Sauce

Chipotle Pot Roast with Spicy Cannellini Beans

Beef Brisket
with Onion and Mushroom Gravy

This meal takes a little more effort than many of the recipes in this book, but it's worth it in the end. Although it takes some time to brown the onions, you do have time while the brisket cooks to get them perfectly caramelized.

Serves
6 to 8

Cooking Time
65 Minutes

Release Method
Natural

1 (3½- to 4-pound) beef brisket

salt and freshly ground black pepper

1 tablespoon olive oil

½ cup red wine

1 cup beef stock

1 teaspoon dried thyme

1 bay leaf

2 cloves garlic, smashed

2 tablespoons brown sugar

1 ounce dried mushrooms

1 tablespoon tomato paste

For the gravy:

2 to 3 tablespoons olive oil

3 large white onions, sliced
(¼-inch slices)

1 pound crimini, shiitake or brown
mushrooms (or a combination), sliced

⅓ cup beef stock

⅓ cup flour

2 tablespoons apple cider vinegar

1. Pre-heat the pressure cooker using the BROWN setting.

2. Season the brisket well with salt and freshly ground black pepper. Add the oil to the pressure cooker and brown the brisket on both sides. Combine the red wine, beef stock, thyme, bay leaf, garlic, brown sugar, dried mushrooms and tomato paste in a bowl, stirring to dissolve the tomato paste. Pour the mixture over the brisket and lock the lid in place.

3. Pressure cook on HIGH for 65 minutes.

4. While the brisket is cooking, start making the gravy. Heat a large skillet or sauté pan over medium heat. Add half the oil and cook the onions until nicely browned – about 20 minutes. Set the onions aside in a bowl. Add the remaining oil and sauté the mushrooms over high heat until nicely browned. Set the mushrooms aside with the onions.

5. When the time is up on the pressure cooker, let the pressure drop NATURALLY and carefully remove the lid. Remove the brisket and bay leaf from the cooker and let the brisket rest for 10 to 15 minutes.

6. In a separate bowl, whisk together the beef stock with the flour, making sure there are no lumps. Whisk this mixture into the hot braising liquid in the pressure cooker. Add the onions and mushrooms to the pressure cooker and bring the mixture to a boil using the BROWN setting. Once at a simmer, turn the cooker off and stir in the vinegar. Slice the brisket into ¼-inch slices and pour the gravy over the top. Serve with mashed potatoes, or the Beets, Potatoes and Bacon (page 185).

You can usually find dried mushrooms in a packet near the produce section of the grocery store. They often come as a variety pack with several different types of mushrooms inside. If not, porcini, shitake, or chanterelles are all great choices.

Beef Brisket
with Dried Plums, Cognac and Cream

Yes, I'm tricking you into trying this recipe with prunes by calling them "dried plums"! Just think of the plums they used to be and enjoy the delicious sweet flavor they bring. This is the longest cooking time in the book, so take a break, close your eyes and let those "visions of sugar plums dance" in your head!

Serves
6 to 8

Cooking Time
75 Minutes

Release Method
Natural

1 cup pitted dried plums (or prunes)

1 cup cognac (or brandy)

1 tablespoon olive oil

1 (3-pound) beef brisket, fat trimmed

salt and freshly ground black pepper

1 onion, chopped

4 cloves garlic, minced

1 large sprig fresh rosemary

1 cup beef stock

¾ cup heavy cream

1. In a small bowl, combine the prunes and cognac, and let the prunes soak for 20 minutes while you prepare the rest of the ingredients and brown the beef.

2. Pre-heat the pressure cooker using the BROWN setting.

3. Add the oil to the cooker. Season the brisket really well with salt and pepper and sear on both sides until nicely brown – 4 minutes a side. Add the onion, garlic and rosemary and pour in the prunes and cognac. Lift the brisket up so that the onion and liquid flow beneath the brisket and bring the liquid to a simmer. Pour in the beef stock and lock the lid in place.

4. Pressure cook on HIGH for 75 minutes.

5. Let the pressure drop NATURALLY and carefully remove the lid. Set the brisket aside, loosely tented with foil, and let it rest for at least 10 minutes. While the brisket is resting, bring the sauce to a simmer using the BROWN setting. Add the heavy cream and season to taste with salt and pepper again. Let the sauce simmer and reduce while you slice the beef into ¼-inch slices. When ready to serve, either return the brisket slices to the sauce to coat, or pour the sauce over the slices. Remember to remove the sprig of rosemary.

You've probably heard the phrase "slice against the grain", but what's "the grain"? You'll see the grain in the brisket pretty easily – it's the lines in the meat. You'll want to slice perpendicular to the lines that you see running in the brisket.

Parmesan Meatballs and Marinara

You have options with this recipe. You can choose to brown the meatballs ahead of time, or you can just pop them into the pressure cooker and cook them right in the sauce. Either way, the meatballs end up extremely tender and moist.

Serves
4

Cooking Time
5 Minutes

Release Method
Natural

1 tablespoon olive oil

1 small onion, very finely chopped

2 cloves garlic, minced

¾ pound ground beef

¾ pound ground pork

¾ cup breadcrumbs

½ cup grated Parmesan cheese

¼ cup finely chopped fresh parsley (plus more for garnish)

1 tablespoon crushed red pepper flakes

2 teaspoons salt

2 eggs, lightly beaten

For the Marinara:

2 tablespoons olive oil

3 cloves garlic, thinly sliced

1 teaspoon dried oregano

½ cup red wine

1 (28-ounce) can tomatoes, chopped

1 (28-ounce) can crushed tomatoes

3 tablespoons tomato paste

1 tablespoon sugar

1 teaspoon salt, plus more for seasoning

1. Pre-heat the pressure cooker using the BROWN setting, or pre-heat a skillet over medium-high heat. Add the oil and cook the onion and garlic until tender, but not browned.

2. Transfer the onion and garlic to a bowl and combine with the meats, breadcrumbs, Parmesan cheese, parsley, crushed red pepper flakes, salt and eggs. Mix together with your hands until everything is evenly combined. Shape the mixture into 36 evenly sized meatballs, no bigger than a golf ball. (A small ice cream scoop works well for this.) Chill the meatballs in the freezer for 15 minutes.

3. Combine the olive oil, garlic and oregano in the pressure cooker. Then, pre-heat the pressure cooker using the BROWN setting. When the garlic is fragrant and just before it turns brown, add the red wine, tomatoes, tomato paste, sugar and salt. Mix well. Transfer the meatballs to the cooker, nestling them down into the sauce. Lock the lid in place.

4. Pressure cook on HIGH for 5 minutes.

5. Let the pressure drop NATURALLY and carefully remove the lid. Serve over pasta or in a hoagie roll topped with cheese for a meatball sub.

Shortcut

It was hard for me to accept that you might be able to cook meatballs without browning them first, but I've tried it both ways, and skipping the browning step is an acceptable shortcut. Just be sure to use very lean ground beef if you decide to go that route.

Corned Beef Reuben Casserole

If you like corned beef and cabbage or if you like a Reuben sandwich, you'll love this blend of the two classics. It makes quite a presentation in a hollowed out bread bowl.

Serves
4

Cooking Time
40 Minutes

Release Method
Quick-release

1 onion, small diced

¾ cup apple cider vinegar

1 tablespoon sugar

1 teaspoon caraway seeds

1 teaspoon salt

1 head green cabbage, shredded

1 (3- to 4-pound) corned beef brisket, with pickling spice packet

1 cup beef stock

1 cup water

2 cups shredded aged Swiss cheese, divided

4 small rye bread boules or large rye rolls

2 tablespoons butter

Thousand Island salad dressing

1. In a large bowl, combine onion, cider vinegar, sugar, caraway seeds, and salt. Add the shredded cabbage and toss to coat. Set aside.

2. Slice the corned beef into ½-inch slices and then cut each slice into 3-inch pieces.

3. Place half the corned beef on the bottom of the pressure cooker. Top with half of the shredded cabbage. Add the rest of corned beef on top of the cabbage and sprinkle the pickling spice over the meat. Finally, add the rest of the cabbage and its juice. Pour the beef stock and water into the cooker and lock the lid in place.

4. Pressure on HIGH for 40 minutes.

5. While the corned beef and cabbage are cooking, cut out a well in the center of each roll and set the rolls aside on a cookie sheet. Crumble the tops and insides of the rolls into coarse bread-crumbs. Melt the butter in a skillet over medium heat and add the breadcrumbs, cooking for a few minutes or until the breadcrumbs are lightly browned and toasted. Set the toasted crumbs aside.

6. When the time on the pressure cooker is almost up, pre-heat the oven to 350ºF.

7. Release the pressure using the QUICK-RELEASE method and carefully remove the lid. Sprinkle half of the Swiss cheese into the cooker, stir a few times and let the cheese melt into the hot liquid. With a slotted spoon, fill the wells of the rolls with the corned beef and cabbage mixture. Top with some Thousand Island dressing and divide the remaining Swiss cheese over each roll. Sprinkle the toasted breadcrumbs on top of the cheese.

8. Place in a 350º F oven for about 8 minutes until the cheese has melted and bread is warm and crispy. Serve immediately.

Nothing beats the presentation of this casserole in a hollowed out bread bowl, but it does take time. Instead, toast some rye bread slices, layer the corned beef and cabbage, Thousand Island dressing, Swiss cheese and breadcrumbs on top and pop it under the broiler for a couple of minutes.

Beef Braciola
with Mushrooms

Braciola is an Italian American dish known in Italy as Involtini. It is made up of thin slices of beef wrapped around a cheese and breadcrumb filling, fried and then cooked in a marinara sauce, which can then be used to top pasta.

Serves
4

Cooking Time
20 Minutes

Release Method
Natural

1½-pound beef top round, sliced into 8 slices (about 4-inches x 6-inches and ½-inch thick)

salt and lots of freshly ground black pepper

2 tablespoons olive oil

2 cloves garlic, minced

¼ cup pinenuts

1 cup dried breadcrumbs

¾ cup grated Pecorino cheese

¼ cup chopped fresh parsley

½ cup sun-dried tomatoes, chopped

2 tablespoons olive oil

1 onion, chopped

2 cloves garlic, minced

6 ounces brown mushrooms, sliced

1 teaspoon dried oregano

3 tablespoons tomato paste

1 cup red wine

1 cup chicken stock

1 (28-ounce) can chopped tomatoes

1 (28-ounce) can crushed tomatoes

1. Lay the slices of beef out on a flat surface and season well with salt and freshly ground black pepper. Pre-heat a skillet on the stovetop on medium-high heat. Add the olive oil and sauté the garlic and pinenuts together. Just before the garlic starts to turn brown, remove the pan from the heat, add the breadcrumbs and toss. Transfer the mixture to a mixing bowl and add the Pecorino cheese, parsley and sun-dried tomatoes. Place a rectangular mound of the filling on each of the beef slices and roll the beef up, tucking the sides in as you roll (sort of like a burrito). Secure each roll by weaving a toothpick through the end of the meat.

2. Pre-heat the pressure cooker using the BROWN setting. Add the olive oil and sear the beef rolls, browning on all sides. Remove the beef to a side plate. Add the onion, garlic and mushrooms to the cooker and sauté until the vegetables start to become tender – about 5 minutes. Add the oregano and tomato paste, stir and cook for a minute or two. Add the wine, bring to a simmer and then add the chicken stock and tomatoes. Season with salt and freshly ground black pepper. Nestle the browned beef rolls into the sauce and lock the lid in place.

3. Pressure cook on HIGH for 20 minutes.

4. Let the pressure drop NATURALLY and carefully remove the lid. Transfer the beef roles to a platter and spoon the sauce over the top.

Shortcut

Ask your butcher for pre-cut braciole (the slices of beef top round) at the meat counter in your grocery store. Braciole can also be called rouladen or involtini. Getting the meat pre-sliced is key to making this recipe a breeze.

Sweet Vidalia Onion Joes

This, of course, is a riff on traditional Sloppy Joes, adding sweet Vidalia onion to the mix, along with a little brown sugar and the secret ingredient – balsamic vinegar. The result is a slightly sweeter version of a dish everyone of my age remembers enjoying as a kid.

Serves
4 to 6

Cooking Time
10 Minutes

Release Method
Combo

1½ pounds lean ground beef

1 tablespoon vegetable oil

1 large Vidalia (or other sweet) onion, finely chopped

2 cloves garlic, minced

1 teaspoon dried oregano

2 tablespoons brown sugar

1 tablespoon balsamic vinegar

2 tablespoons tomato ketchup

1 (14-ounce) can tomatoes, chopped or crushed by hand

½ cup beef stock

1 teaspoon salt

freshly ground black pepper

4 to 6 Kaiser rolls, Ciabatta, hamburger buns or potato rolls

1. Pre-heat the pressure cooker using the BROWN setting.

2. Brown the beef, stirring to break the ground beef up into small pieces. Transfer the beef to a bowl with a slotted spoon, draining away and discarding all the fat.

3. Add the oil to the cooker, sauté the onion, garlic and oregano and cook until the onion starts to soften and brown slightly – about 8 minutes. Add the brown sugar, balsamic vinegar, tomato ketchup and tomatoes and stir well. Return the beef to the cooker, pour in the beef stock, season with salt and freshly ground black pepper and lock the lid in place.

4. Pressure cook on HIGH for 10 minutes.

5. Let the pressure drop NATURALLY for 10 minutes. Release any residual pressure with the QUICK-RELEASE method and carefully remove the lid. Season to taste again with salt and freshly ground black pepper and serve over the bread rolls.

 Did You Know...?

The secret to a good Sloppy Joe rests with the bun you choose to put underneath. The bun should definitely absorb all the juice and flavor from the meat, but you also want it to hold its shape somewhat, and not disintegrate. I prefer a Ciabatta or Kaiser roll, but hamburger buns or potato rolls will do the job too.

Turkish Beef and Eggplant Moussaka

Moussaka is most commonly thought of as the Greek potato or eggplant-based dish that is layered and baked with Béchamel sauce on top. In Turkey, however, moussaka is not a layered dish, but is prepared by sautéing eggplant and beef and topping it with tomatoes and/or peppers. In this recipe, you'll make a stew with ground beef, eggplant, tomatoes, potatoes and zucchini all in one pot, incorporating the flavors of moussaka.

Serves
6 to 8

Cooking Time
10 Minutes

Release Method
Quick-release

2 pounds lean ground beef

1 tablespoon olive oil

1 onion, chopped (about 1 cup)

2 cloves garlic, minced

2 teaspoons dried oregano

1 teaspoon ground cinnamon

¼ teaspoon ground nutmeg

½ cup red wine

½ cup beef stock

1 (28-ounce) can tomatoes, chopped

2 tablespoons tomato paste

2 teaspoons salt

freshly ground black pepper

2 Russet potatoes, peeled and cubed (1-inch cubes)

1 medium eggplant, cubed (1-inch cubes)

3 zucchini, cubed (1-inch cubes)

2 tablespoons chopped fresh oregano

crumbled feta cheese

1. Pre-heat the pressure cooker using the BROWN setting.

2. Brown the beef in two batches until all the fat has been rendered. Remove the beef with a slotted spoon and set aside. Drain away and discard the fat.

3. Add the olive oil to the cooker and sauté the onion and garlic for 3 to 4 minutes. Stir in the dried oregano, cinnamon and nutmeg and cook for another minute. Stir in the red wine, beef stock, tomatoes, tomato paste, salt and pepper. Return the meat to the cooker, add the potato, eggplant and zucchini, stir well and lock the lid in place.

4. Pressure cook on HIGH for 10 minutes.

5. Release the pressure using the QUICK-RELEASE method and carefully remove the lid. Season again to taste with salt and freshly ground black pepper. Serve over egg noodles or rice, garnished with some chopped fresh oregano and crumbled feta cheese.

Dress It Up

If you want to make this into more of a traditional Turkish moussaka, transfer the finished product to a casserole dish (or individual gratin dishes), layer some slices of tomato on top and bake in a 350°F oven for about 30 minutes, topping with the feta cheese at the end.

Jiggs Dinner

One of my favorite vacations was a short week in Newfoundland, Canada's easternmost province, where Jiggs dinner is the traditional Sunday dinner. It is very much like a New England boiled dinner, but with a bag of yellow split peas cooked in the pot. It is named after a cartoon character in George McManus' cartoon "Bringing up Father". Jiggs was the main character who was always eating corned beef and cabbage. My favorite part of the meal is the split peas cooked in the delicious salty broth and then smashed with butter, salt and pepper. I could eat those all by themselves!

Serves
4 to 6

Cooking Time
55 + 8 + 5 Minutes

Release Method
Combo

1 (3½-pound) corned beef brisket (or salt beef if you can find it!)

4 cups beef stock

2 bay leaves

1 onion, quartered

3 cloves garlic, smashed

1 cup dried yellow split peas

cheesecloth or a "pudding bag"

6 large carrots, halved

6 medium white potatoes, halved

1 small to medium head cabbage, cut into 6 wedges

2 tablespoons butter

salt and freshly ground black pepper

whole-grain mustard

pickles

1. Cut the beef into large chunks that will fit easily into your pressure cooker. Pour the beef stock into the cooker with your chuncks of beef and add the bay leaves, onion and garlic. Lock the lid in place.

2. Cook on HIGH pressure for 55 minutes.

3. Let the pressure drop NATURALLY and carefully remove the lid. Transfer the beef chunks to a serving platter and tent with aluminum foil.

4. Place the dried split peas into a pudding bag, or wrap them in the cheesecloth, tying the cheesecloth loosely so that the peas have room to expand. Push the bag down into the broth. Add the carrots, potatoes and cabbage to the cooker, and lock the lid in place.

5. Pressure cook on HIGH pressure for 8 minutes.

6. Release the pressure using the QUICK-RELEASE method and carefully remove the lid. Remove the vegetables and transfer to a serving platter. Leave the pudding bag in the cooker, lock the lid in place and pressure cook on HIGH for an additional 5 minutes.

7. Release the pressure using the QUICK-RELEASE method and carefully remove the lid. Transfer the cooked split peas to a bowl. Remove the cheesecloth and discard. Mash the peas with a wooden spoon, stirring in the butter and season with salt and lots of freshly ground black pepper.

8. Slice the beef and transfer to the platter with the vegetables. Serve with the peas, mustard and pickles.

Jiggs dinner is traditionally made with salt beef, but because it is not always easy to find, this version uses corned beef brisket. If you do find salt beef, remember to soak the beef in cold water for 8 to 10 hours before preparing the recipe above.

Hunter's Beef Stew

This recipe is really a version of beef Cacciatore – Italian for "hunter". It's an earthy stew with mushrooms, peppers and carrots, but what makes it really special is the horseradish that is stirred in at the end, giving it a "je ne sais quoi" quality.

Serves
4

Cooking Time
20 Minutes

Release Method
Natural

1 tablespoon vegetable oil

2 pounds beef stew meat, trimmed of fat and cut into bite-sized pieces

salt and freshly ground black pepper

1 onion, chopped into ½-inch pieces

3 carrots, chopped into 1-inch chunks (about 3 cups)

2 cloves garlic, minced

1 green bell pepper, chopped into 1-inch chunks

1 red bell pepper, chopped into 1-inch chunks

8 ounces button mushrooms, quartered

1 teaspoon dried thyme

1 sprig of fresh rosemary

½ cup red wine

1½ cups beef stock

2 tablespoons Worcestershire sauce

1 (14-ounce) can of tomatoes, diced

2 tablespoons prepared horseradish (not horseradish sauce)

fresh thyme, for garnish

1. Pre-heat the pressure cooker using the BROWN setting.

2. Add the oil to the cooker and brown the beef in batches, seasoning with salt and pepper and setting the browned beef aside in a bowl. Add the onions and carrots to the cooker and sauté until the onion starts to become tender – about 5 minutes. Add the garlic, peppers, mushrooms, thyme and rosemary and stir well. Cook for an additional minute or two. Pour in the red wine, beef stock, Worcestershire sauce and tomatoes, and bring to a boil. Return the beef to the cooker and stir well, doing your best to submerge the beef in the liquid. Lock the lid in place.

3. Pressure cook on HIGH for 20 minutes.

4. Let the pressure drop NATURALLY and carefully remove the lid. Stir in the horseradish and season to taste with salt and freshly ground black pepper. Don't forget to remove the sprig of rosemary before serving with some fresh thyme leaves on top.

Beef Dip Sandwiches

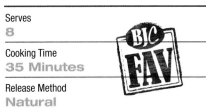

When I was a kid, I LOVED a beef dip sandwich and can remember ordering it many times on those occasions when I was out to lunch with my mum. It's the simplest of sandwiches, but somehow it's made fun by having the jus to dip the sandwich in. It's not just a kid thing though, because I still love a good beef dip sandwich today!

Serves
8

Cooking Time
35 Minutes

Release Method
Natural

1 (3-pound) beef chuck roast

salt and lots of freshly ground black pepper

2 tablespoons olive oil

3 onions, thinly sliced

2 cloves garlic, smashed

1 teaspoon brown sugar

1 teaspoon dried thyme

½ teaspoon dried rosemary

1 bay leaf

3 cups good quality beef stock

8 white Italian bread rolls

½ cup horseradish

¼ cup sour cream

1. Pre-heat the pressure cooker using the BROWN setting.

2. Season the beef roast with salt and pepper. Add the oil and brown the beef well on all sides. Take some time with this step and try not to be impatient. Remove the roast to a side plate. Add the onion, garlic, brown sugar and dried herbs and cook until the onions start to brown. Add a little beef stock, stir and continue to brown until the onions are golden – about 15 minutes. Pour in the remaining beef stock, scraping the bottom of the cooker to stir up any of the brown bits, and return the roast to the cooker. Lock the lid in place.

3. Pressure cook on HIGH for 35 minutes.

4. Let the pressure drop NATURALLY and carefully remove the lid. Remove the roast to a resting plate and loosely tent with foil for at least 10 minutes. While the roast is resting, return the cooker to the BROWN setting and let the onion jus reduce to concentrate the flavors. Season to taste with salt and pepper. Strain the jus into a fat separator and let the fat rise to the surface. Pour the flavorful jus out into ramekins and discard the fat and bay leaf.

5. Combine the horseradish and sour cream and spread the mixture on each side of the rolls. Thinly slice the beef and fill the sandwiches with the beef and onions. Serve each sandwich with a little ramekin of jus for dipping.

Did You Know...?

Having a flavorful jus is critical to the success of this simple sandwich. So, use the best quality beef stock you can. You can also fortify the stock by adding beef bones to the liquid as it simmers and cooks the beef.

Beef Bites

Beef (especially big cuts of beef) really benefits from time in a pressure cooker. It's possible to take large cuts of beef that are often tough, but very flavorful (and usually relatively inexpensive) and make them tender, juicy and delicious under pressure. Even stew meat that can be terribly tough and chewy is transformed in the pressure cooker and becomes incredibly succulent and tender in a fraction of the time it would take on the stovetop or in the oven. It's a minor miracle!

Brown first.	Browning the beef first is not just for looks. Having some color on the meat, whether it's a large roast or small cubes in a stew will also add flavor and enhance the overall result of the dish. Browning first also helps to render away some of the fat of the beef, allowing you to discard it before incorporating it into the recipe. This is especially important for recipes using ground beef.
Let it drop Naturally!	The release method is really important for beef. Always use a natural release method for pieces of beef, whether stew chunks or large roasts. Letting the pressure drop on its own, or naturally allows the meat to cool to an edible temperature more gradually, and the result is a more tender piece of beef. For ground beef, this is not as important and the quick-release method can be used.
Thickening Strategies.	When you've finished cooking beef in the pressure cooker, you're left with a braising liquid that is full of flavor and can make a delicious sauce if you thicken it. There are several ways to do this. No matter which method you use, always bring the liquid to a boil after adding the thickener to achieve the right consistency.
Whisk in Flour.	This can work to thicken a sauce in a pinch, but you run a very high risk of having lumps of flour in the final dish.
Make a Roux.	A roux is equal parts butter and flour, cooked. You can make a roux in a saucepan on the stovetop and then whisk the braising liquid to the saucepan.
Try a Beurre Manié.	A beurre manié is equal parts butter and flour, uncooked. You might find a slight starchy taste to a beurre manié since the flour doesn't get cooked, but it's easier to put together than a roux. The butter needs to be soft and at room temperature. Just combine the two ingredients into a paste and whisk that paste into the braising liquid.
Cornmeal.	Whisking cornmeal into a dish can also help to thicken the liquid, but will also give a slight corn flavor so make sure that's what you want. It's a great way to thicken chilies.
Potato Flakes.	Potato flakes also absorb water and therefore thicken liquids without altering the flavor too much.
Use a Slurry.	A slurry can give a sheen to the finished sauce as well as thicken it to the right consistency. Dissolve cornstarch in a couple tablespoons of cold water and then whisk the slurry into the hot liquid to thicken.

Stout-Braised Beef Short Ribs

There's a pleasant bitterness to the sauce for these short ribs, which comes from the stout beer. The recipe calls for you to strain the vegetables out of the braising liquid, which results in a rather elegant sauce. If you like a more rustic meal, leave the vegetables in, but be sure to take the fat off the surface of the braising liquid before serving.

Serves
4 to 6

Cooking Time
55 Minutes

Release Method
Natural

1 tablespoon brown sugar

1 tablespoon paprika

½ teaspoon dry mustard powder

½ teaspoon chili powder

1 tablespoon kosher salt

1 teaspoon coarsely ground black pepper

4 pounds beef short ribs

2 tablespoons olive oil

1 large sweet onion, sliced

2 ribs celery, chopped

1 carrot, chopped

3 cloves garlic, smashed

3 sprigs fresh thyme

1 bay leaf

16 ounces stout beer (coffee stout is especially nice)

1 cup good quality beef stock

1 (14-ounce) can tomatoes, chopped

2 tablespoons tomato paste

1 tablespoon cornstarch

¼ cup heavy cream

½ teaspoon salt

chopped fresh chives (1-inch pieces) for garnish

1. Combine the brown sugar, paprika, dry mustard powder, chili powder, kosher salt and freshly ground black pepper. Rub this spice blend all over the short ribs and let the ribs sit for about 30 minutes while you prepare the rest of the ingredients.

2. Pre-heat the pressure cooker using the BROWN setting.

3. Add the olive oil and when the oil is hot and almost smoking, sear the short ribs in batches, until browned on all sides. Set the browned ribs aside and drain away and discard any fat from the cooker. Add the onion, celery and carrot and cook for 2 to 3 minutes. Add the garlic, thyme, and bay leaf and continue to cook for another minute or two. Add the beer and deglaze the cooker, scraping up any brown bits on the bottom of the pan. Bring the mixture to a simmer. Add the beef stock, tomatoes and tomato paste, stir and return the browned short ribs to the cooker, nestling them into the sauce. Lock the lid in place.

4. Pressure cook on HIGH for 55 minutes.

5. Let the pressure drop NATUALLY and carefully remove the lid. Remove the ribs from the cooker and set aside, loosely covered with foil to rest for at least 5 minutes. While the ribs are resting, strain the sauce into a fat separator, letting the fat rise to the surface. Discard the vegetables. Return 2 cups of the strained and de-fatted sauce to the pressure cooker and return the cooker to the BROWN setting. Whisk together the cornstarch and heavy cream in a small bowl. Whisk this mixture into the simmering sauce and let it come to a boil to thicken. Season to taste with salt and freshly ground black pepper. Return the ribs to the cooker and turn them to coat in this sauce. Serve the ribs over smashed potatoes, spoon a little sauce on top and garnish with chives.

There are two types of beef short ribs, depending on how they are cut by the butcher. "English Style" short ribs are cut parallel to the bone so they have one long rib bone covered with meat. "Flanken Style" short ribs are cut across the bones, creating a piece of meat that has three or four little bones in it. Either cut is suitable for this recipe.

Curried Beef
with Cucumber Yogurt Sauce

A good quality curry powder can have quite a bit of kick to it. That, in addition to the fact that this recipe calls for two full tablespoons of curry powder, can make this a spicy dish. The cucumber yogurt sauce really helps to tame the heat though, so don't be afraid!

Serves
4

Cooking Time
20 Minutes

Release Method
Combo

3 tablespoons vegetable oil, divided

2 pounds beef stew meat, trimmed of fat and cubed

1 onion, chopped (about 1 cup)

2 cloves garlic, minced

2 inches fresh ginger, peeled and minced

2 tablespoons good quality curry powder

1 (14-ounce) can tomatoes, diced

1 cup beef stock

1 pound Yukon Gold potatoes, diced (a scant 3 cups or 2 medium sized potatoes)

salt and freshly ground black pepper

½ English cucumber, grated (1 cup)

½ clove garlic, finely minced

1 cup plain yogurt

1 tablespoon olive oil

¼ - ½ cup chopped fresh cilantro (or parsley)

1. Pre-heat the pressure cooker using the BROWN setting.

2. Add a tablespoon of oil and brown the stew meat in batches, adding more oil as needed. Set the meat aside in a bowl. Add the onion and sauté until the onion starts to become tender – about 5 minutes. Add the garlic, ginger and curry powder and continue to cook for another minute or two. Add the tomatoes and beef stock, return the browned beef to the cooker and stir in the potatoes. Season with salt and freshly ground black pepper and lock the lid in place.

3. Pressure cook on HIGH for 20 minutes.

4. While the curry is cooking, prepare the cucumber yogurt sauce. Place the grated cucumber in a strainer and sprinkle with salt. Let this drain while the curry is cooking. Meanwhile, combine the garlic, yogurt and oil in a bowl. Just before serving, stir the cucumber into the yogurt sauce and season to taste with freshly ground black pepper.

5. Let the pressure drop NATURALLY for 15 minutes. Then, release any remaining pressure with the QUICK-RELEASE method and carefully remove the lid. Season the curry again to taste with salt and pepper. Sprinkle the cilantro on top and spoon a dollop of the cucumber yogurt sauce in the middle. Serve with rice or some naan bread.

 Did You Know....?

Curry powder is not something commonly used in India. There, cooks mix spices to create the curry flavors they are looking for, and each blend is as different as the next. Curry powder was a western invention of convenience to make it easier for cooks unfamiliar with the wide variety of Indian spices. As such, the flavors of curry powders vary from brand to brand, so find one that you like and stick to it, or... experiment a little and vary your curries from time to time.

Chipotle Pot Roast
with Spicy Cannellini Beans

Here's a nice variation on a pot roast, incorporating beans into the braising liquid instead of the traditional vegetables. It's as tender as a traditional Sunday pot roast, but with a spicy kick at the end!

Serves
6 to 8

Cooking Time
60 Minutes

Release Method
Natural

2 teaspoons salt

2 teaspoons chili powder

½ teaspoon smoked paprika

1 (3- to 3½-pound) boneless chuck roast

1 tablespoon vegetable oil

2 red onions, sliced

2 cloves garlic, smashed

1 teaspoon dried oregano

1 chipotle pepper in adobo, chopped

2 teaspoons of adobo sauce

1 (12-ounce) bottle ale beer

1 (14-ounce) can chopped tomatoes

1 cup beef stock

2 tablespoons brown sugar

1 bay leaf

1 cup dried white cannellini beans

¼ cup chopped fresh parsley

1. Pre-heat the pressure cooker using the BROWN setting.

2. Combine the salt, chili powder and smoked paprika. Season the roast on all sides with the mixture. Add the oil to the cooker and brown the roast on all sides. Transfer the roast to a resting plate.

3. Add the onion, garlic, oregano, chipotle pepper and adobo sauce to the cooker and cook for a minute or two. Pour in the ale and using a wooden spoon, scrape up any brown bits that have formed on the bottom of the cooker. Bring to a simmer. Add the tomatoes and beef stock to the cooker, along with the brown sugar, bay leaf and cannellini beans. Return the browned beef to the cooker and lock the lid in place.

4. Pressure cook on HIGH for 60 minutes.

5. Let the pressure drop NATURALLY and carefully remove the lid. Transfer the roast to a side plate and tent with foil to rest for at least 10 minutes. Remove the bay leaf and skim the fat from the surface of the braising liquid. Season the beans to taste with salt and pepper and spoon the beans and juice over the roast. Serve with some mashed potatoes or sweet potatoes and garnish with chopped fresh parsley.

Did You Know...?

Chipotle peppers are dried and smoked Jalapeño peppers. They usually come in a can, packed in adobo sauce and can be found in the Mexican or ethnic section of the grocery store.

Pork

Pork Chops with Orange Marmalade Glaze

Dry-Rubbed Baby Back Ribs with BBQ Sauce

Dry-Rubbed Baby Back Ribs with Cherry Chipotle Sauce

Dry-Rubbed Baby Back Ribs with Sweet and Sour Sauce

Country Style Pork Ribs with Mustard and Cream

Pork Stew with Cabbage and Tomatoes

Pork Carnitas

Pot Roast Shoulder of Pork with Apple Gravy

Keilbasa and Sauerkraut and Apples

Madeira Ham with Apricots

Pork Chops with Artichokes, Capers, Sundried Tomatoes and Lemons

Pork Chops
with Orange Marmalade Glaze

These pork chops have a slightly sweet Asian flavor. The cooking time is short, but make sure you let the pressure drop naturally for a really tender chop. This recipe calls for chops that are at least one inch thick. If your chops are thinner than one inch, drop the cooking time by one or two minutes.

Serves
4

Cooking Time
4 Minutes

Release Method
Natural

4 boneless center cut pork chops, at least 1-inch thick

salt and freshly ground black pepper

1 teaspoon vegetable oil

1 onion, chopped into 1-inch chunks

½ cup chicken stock

1½ cups baby cut carrots, whole

1 can sliced water chestnuts

1 orange, sliced

½ cup + 2 tablespoons orange juice

1 (12-ounce) jar orange marmalade

2 teaspoons soy sauce

1 tablespoon honey

1½ cups sugar snap peas

1. Pre-heat the pressure cooker using the BROWN setting. Season the pork chops with salt and freshly ground black pepper. Add the oil and brown the pork chops on both sides. Remove the browned chops and set aside.

2. Add the onion to the cooker and sauté until the onion starts to brown and soften – about 8 minutes. Add the chicken stock and stir, scraping up any brown bits on the bottom of cooker. Add the carrots, water chestnuts, orange slices and ½ cup of orange juice to the cooker. Stir to combine, pushing the slices down into the liquid. Return the browned pork chops to the cooker, placing them on top of the vegetables and liquid. Turn the cooker off.

3. In a small bowl whisk together orange marmalade, soy sauce, honey, and two tablespoons of orange juice. Spoon half of this mixture onto the pork chops and reserve the other half to add to the sauce at the end. Lock the lid in place.

4. Pressure cook on HIGH for 4 minutes.

5. Let the pressure drop NATURALLY and carefully remove the lid. Transfer the pork chops and vegetables to a platter and cover loosely with foil. Reserve half a cup of the braising liquid from the pressure cooker and discard the rest. Return the pressure cooker to the BROWN setting. Add reserved braising liquid, sugar snap peas and reserved orange marmalade mixture. Bring sauce to boil and simmer until it thickens – about 3 minutes. Serve the pork chops and vegetables over rice, pouring the sauce evenly over the top.

Dry-Rubbed Baby Back Ribs with BBQ Sauce

This is my favorite method of cooking ribs in the pressure cooker. The spice rub applied to the ribs before browning gives them color and flavor and steaming the ribs over a flavorful broth makes them super tender without washing away the flavor. The finishing touch is transforming the flavorful broth into a sauce to slather on the ribs at the end. Here you have three sauces to choose from.

Serves
4

Cooking Time
30 Minutes

Release Method
Natural

2 teaspoons smoked paprika

1 teaspoon dry mustard powder

2 teaspoons dried oregano

2 teaspoons dried thyme

1 teaspoon chili powder

2 teaspoons salt

4 pounds baby back ribs (about 2 racks), cut into 3-rib sections

1 to 2 tablespoons olive or vegetable oil

½ onion, chopped

1 bay leaf

1 cup beef stock

Sauce:

1 cup tomato ketchup

2 tablespoons molasses

1 tablespoon cider vinegar

1 tablespoon tomato paste

½ teaspoon soy sauce

1. Combine the first 6 ingredients to make the dry rub spice blend, and rub the spice blend all over the rib sections.

2. Pre-heat the pressure cooker using the BROWN setting.

3. Add the oil to the cooker and brown the ribs in batches. (Alternately, you can do this in a pan on the stovetop.) Remove the ribs and set aside. Add the onion and bay leaf to the cooker and sauté until the onion starts to soften – about 5 minutes. Pour in the beef stock and place a steam rack in the bottom of the cooker. Place the browned ribs on the rack, and lock the lid in place. It's ok to pile the ribs on top of each other in an uneven manner, or to stand the ribs up vertically.

4. Pressure cook on HIGH for 30 minutes.

5. While the ribs are cooking, combine the ketchup, molasses, cider vinegar, tomato paste and soy sauce in a small bowl.

6. Let the pressure drop NATURALLY and carefully remove the lid. Remove the ribs and let them rest on a side plate. While the ribs are resting, remove the steam rack and pour the ketchup mixture into the cooker with the cooking liquid. Return the cooker to the BROWN setting. Simmer the sauce ingredients for about 5 minutes and then return the ribs to the sauce to coat and serve.

Baby back ribs are leaner and more tender than spare ribs. They are also shorter and fit more easily into most pressure cookers. You can absolutely try this rib-cooking technique with spare ribs, however. Just increase the cooking time to 45 minutes.

Dry-Rubbed Baby Back Ribs with Cherry Chipotle Sauce

2 chipotle peppers in Adobo sauce

2 teaspoons Adobo sauce

1 (13-ounce) jar cherry preserves

1 cup tomato ketchup

1. Follow the directions for the Dry-Rubbed Baby Back Ribs with BBQ Sauce through step 4.

2. While the ribs are cooking, chop the chipotle peppers very finely with a knife. Mix the chopped chipotle peppers, cherry preserves, and ketchup in a small bowl.

3. Let the pressure drop NATURALLY and carefully remove the lid. Remove the ribs and let them rest on a side plate. While the ribs are resting, remove the steam rack and pour the sauce ingredients into the cooker with the cooking liquid. Return the cooker to the BROWN setting. Simmer the sauce ingredients for about 5 to 8 minutes until it starts to thicken and then return the ribs to the sauce to coat and serve.

Dry-Rubbed Baby Back Ribs with Sweet and Sour Sauce

2 tablespoons minced green bell pepper

1 cup tomato ketchup

1 cup brown sugar

¼ cup apple cider vinegar

1 tablespoon soy sauce

1 tablespoon Worcestershire sauce

½ cup crushed pineapple, drained

½ teaspoon dry mustard powder

½ teaspoon freshly ground black pepper

1. Follow the directions for the Dry-Rubbed Baby Back Ribs with BBQ Sauce through step 4.

2. While the ribs are cooking, combine the green pepper, ketchup, brown sugar, cider vinegar, soy sauce, Worcestershire sauce, crushed pineapple, dry mustard powder, and black pepper in a small bowl.

3. Let the pressure drop NATURALLY and carefully remove the lid. Remove the ribs and let them rest on a side plate. While the ribs are resting, remove the steam rack and pour the sauce ingredients into the cooker with the cooking liquid. Return the cooker to the BROWN setting. Simmer the sauce ingredients for about 5 to 8 minutes until sauce thickens and then return the ribs to the sauce to coat and serve.

Pork Report

Pork has earned a bad reputation over the years. It became the "other white meat" that was all too often over-cooked and dry. Now, the pressure cooker is here to redeem pork's image! Cooking pork under pressure not only helps make it tender, but helps keep it moist too. The pressure cooker traps all the steam and flavor inside the cooker, so the pork doesn't have a chance to dry out and just becomes more flavorful.

Any cut will do!	You can cook any cut of pork in a pressure cooker if you adjust the time accordingly, but my favorite cuts to cook under pressure are ribs (spare or baby back) and shoulder (or Boston butt). Loin roasts, pork chops and country style ribs also work really well.
Chop chop! What types of chops to use in a pressure cooker.	You have basically four types of pork chops to choose from. Two of these – the shoulder chop and the sirloin chops – are tough chops that benefit from braising or pressure-cooking. The other two types – rib chop and loin chops – can also work really well in a pressure cooker, but do need to be at least 1-inch and preferably 1½-inches thick. If your chops are thinner than an inch, reduce the cooking time by a couple of minutes.
Baby back ribs or spare ribs?	Fear not – both types of ribs can be delicious out of a pressure cooker! The difference is that baby back ribs tend to be smaller, more tender and leaner than spare ribs. Spare ribs, on the other hand, are often more flavorful than baby back ribs, but take a little more time to become as tender. You pick the rib and time accordingly – 30 minutes for baby back ribs and 45 minutes for spare ribs.
Browning will add flavor and eye-appeal.	Everything looks better with a little color! More importantly, browning pork ahead of cooking it under pressure will add flavor, especially if it is rubbed with a spice blend first.
Let it drop Naturally!	The release method is as important for pork as it is for beef. Always let the pressure drop on its own, or naturally when cooking pork. This will let the fibers in the pork relax more gradually and the result will be a more tender piece of meat. I sometimes make an exception for sausages, releasing the pressure using the quick-release method to stop the cooking process. This can cause the sausage casing to burst a little, however, so if you're going for looks, stick with the natural release.

Country Style Pork Ribs
with Mustard and Cream

Though the name of this recipe sounds rustic, it can actually pass for an elegant dinner. The sauce is a smooth, but relatively thin sauce that coats the ribs nicely and would be delicious over potatoes too. If you'd prefer a thicker gravy-like sauce, simply whisk in some butter and flour mixed together (a beurre manié) at the end.

Serves
4 to 6

Cooking Time
25 Minutes

Release Method
Natural

2 teaspoons smoked paprika

1 teaspoon dry mustard powder

2 teaspoons dried thyme

2 teaspoons salt

freshly ground black pepper

3 pounds country style pork ribs

2 tablespoons olive oil

2 shallots, minced

2 cloves garlic, smashed

2 tablespoons apple cider vinegar

½ cup chicken stock

¾ cup heavy cream

2 tablespoons whole-grain mustard

2 tablespoons chopped fresh thyme

salt and freshly ground black pepper

1. Combine the paprika, mustard powder, dried thyme, salt and freshly ground black pepper. Rub this spice mix onto the ribs and set them aside while you prepare the rest of the ingredients (or leave it on to marinate for up to 24 hours).

2. Pre-heat the pressure cooker using the BROWN setting.

3. Add the oil and brown the ribs in batches on all sides. Set the browned ribs aside. Add the shallots and garlic to the cooker and sauté for 2 to 3 minutes. Add the vinegar, stock, cream and mustard, stir well and return the ribs to the liquid. Lock the lid in place.

4. Pressure cook on HIGH for 25 minutes.

5. Let the pressure drop NATURALLY and carefully remove the lid. Transfer the ribs to a resting plate and loosely tent with foil, for at least 5 minutes. Return the pressure cooker to the BROWN setting and bring the sauce to a simmer. Stir in the fresh thyme. Season to taste with salt and freshly ground black pepper and serve over the ribs.

Country-style ribs are not actually ribs at all! They are cut from the blade end of the pork loin, near the shoulder. As a result, they don't actually contain any rib bones and are meatier than baby back or spare ribs. They are really more like pork chops.

Pork Stew
with Cabbage and Tomatoes

This recipe deserves a more inviting name! Pork and cabbage are a classic combination, but adding the apple and tomato makes it a little different from what you might expect.

Serves
6 to 8

Cooking Time
35 Minutes

Release Method
Natural

2 teaspoons salt

freshly ground black pepper

1 teaspoon dried thyme

1 teaspoon dried oregano

½ teaspoon dried basil

1 (4-pound) shoulder of pork, trimmed of excess fat and cut into 1½- to 2-inch chunks

1 to 2 tablespoons olive oil

2 onions, sliced

4 large carrots, peeled and cut into 3 large chunks each (or baby cut carrots)

4 cloves garlic, smashed

2 large tomatoes, cut into large chunks

1 bay leaf

1 small cabbage (or ½ large cabbage), cut into wedges (1-inch thick at widest point)

2 apples, peeled and diced

1 (24-ounce) jar marinara sauce

1 cup chicken stock

¼ cup chopped fresh parsley

1. Combine the salt, pepper, thyme, oregano and basil and toss the chunks of pork in this spice mixture.

2. Pre-heat the pressure cooker using the BROWN setting.

3. Add the oil and brown the pork in batches. Set the pork aside and add the onion, carrots and garlic to the cooker. Sauté until the onion starts to soften slightly – about 5 minutes. Add the tomatoes and bay leaf and return the browned pork to the cooker. Place a layer of cabbage wedges on top of the pork and scatter the diced apple over the top. Repeat with the remaining cabbage and diced apple. Combine the marinara sauce and the chicken stock and pour the mixture over the top of everything. Lock the lid in place.

4. Pressure cook on HIGH for 35 minutes.

5. Let the pressure drop NATURALLY and carefully remove the lid. Season the stew to taste with salt and pepper. Serve in a deep bowl over rice and sprinkle chopped fresh parsley on top.

Did You Know...?

Pork shoulder is also called pork butt, or Boston butt. That's not very intuitive in our modern day language, but the word "butt" actually derives from Old English meaning "an extremity" and usually the "widest part". On a pig, the widest part is actually the shoulder, not the rear end!

Pork Carnitas

This is one of my favorite recipes in the book. It's delicious and very versatile. For me, a batch of carnitas will last several meals and can be made into quesadillas, burritos, tacos, salads, and even an open-faced sandwich. Skimming off the fat and reducing the braising liquid also makes a terrific sauce to moisten the meat in whatever you choose to make.

Serves
8 to 10

Cooking Time
55 Minutes

Release Method
Natural

3 pounds boneless pork shoulder

2 teaspoons dried oregano

1 teaspoon ground cumin

½ teaspoon ground cayenne pepper

½ teaspoon ground coriander

½ teaspoon ground cinnamon

2 teaspoons salt

2 tablespoons vegetable oil,
plus more for frying before serving

2 onions, cut into wedges

4 cloves garlic, smashed

2 Jalapeño peppers, sliced (leave the seeds in if you like really spicy foods)

1 cup beef stock

2 large oranges

flour tortillas, salsa, guacamole, grated Cheddar cheese, sour cream, cilantro (for serving)

1. Cut the pork shoulder into chunks that will fit into your pressure cooker. Combine the oregano, cumin, cayenne pepper, coriander, cinnamon and salt and rub the spice mix on the pork chunks.

2. Pre-heat the pressure cooker using the BROWN setting.

3. Add the oil to the cooker and brown the pork chunks on all sides. Remove the browned pork and set aside. Add the onion, garlic and Jalapeño peppers and cook for a minute or two. Return the pork chunks to the cooker and add the beef stock. Cut the oranges in half, squeeze the juice all over the pork chunks and throw the orange halves into the cooker. The pork should only be partially covered in liquid. Lock the lid in place.

4. Pressure cook on HIGH for 55 minutes.

5. Let the pressure drop NATURALLY and carefully remove the lid. Transfer the pork chunks to a resting plate and let them rest for at least 10 minutes. Shred the pork chunks completely, using two forks. Reserve the shredded pork until you are ready to serve.

6. To serve the carnitas, heat a skillet over medium-high heat. Add some oil to the skillet and fry the shredded pork in batches until it has crispy parts. Serve the crisped pork in taco shells or flour tortillas with your favorite toppings – salsa, guacamole, tomatoes, cheese, sour cream and some cilantro.

Did You Know...?

Most of the spicy heat of a Jalapeño is in its seeds. If you like spicy foods, leave the seeds in the recipe. Otherwise, remove the seeds and slice up just the flesh of the chili pepper.

Pot Roast Shoulder of Pork with Apple Gravy

This was one of the first recipes I wrote for this book. My good friend, David Venable had been talking and talking about his mother's pork pot roast and I felt inspired. It does take a little effort to make the gravy at the end, but it's so worth it!

Serves
6

Cooking Time
55 Minutes

Release Method
Natural

BIG FAV

1 (4-pound) shoulder of pork, trimmed of excess fat

salt and lots of freshly ground black pepper

1 teaspoon dried thyme

½ teaspoon dried rosemary

olive oil

1 onion, cut into wedges

3 large carrots, peeled and cut into 3 large chunks each

12 fingerling potatoes (or baby potatoes)

1 apple, peeled, cored and quartered

1 bay leaf

1 cup Madeira wine

1½ cups chicken stock

¾ cup apple cider or apple juice, divided

2 tablespoons butter

¼ cup flour

¼ cup heavy cream

2 teaspoons chopped fresh thyme leaves, plus sprigs for garnish

1. Trim the excess fat from the shoulder of pork, but be sure to leave some on the roast. Cut the pork shoulder into the largest manageable chunks that will fit into the pressure cooker – probably two chunks. Season the pork very well on all sides with the salt, pepper, thyme and rosemary.

2. Pre-heat the pressure cooker using the BROWN setting.

3. Add the oil and brown the pork well on all sides. Take some time with this step and try not to be impatient. Add the onion, carrots, potatoes and apple, scattering them around and on top of the pork. Season again with salt and pepper, add the bay leaf and Madeira wine, and bring to a simmer. Add the chicken stock and ½ cup of the apple cider, and lock the lid in place.

4. Pressure cook on HIGH for 55 minutes.

5. Let the pressure drop NATURALLY and carefully remove the lid. Remove the pork, onions, carrots and potatoes and place them in a bowl while you make the gravy.

6. Make the gravy by straining the cooking liquid into a fat separator. Press as much of the cooked apple through the strainer into the cooking liquid as possible. Let the cooking liquid settle so the fat rises to the surface.

7. Return the cooker to the BROWN setting and add the butter. When the butter has melted, stir in the flour and cook for a minute or two. Whisk in the remaining apple cider and the cooking liquid from the fat separator, trying not to add any of the fat. Bring the mixture to a boil to thicken. Season to taste with salt (about 1½ teaspoons) and pepper. Stir in the heavy cream and the thyme leaves. Return the pork and vegetables to the cooker and let everything sit together until you are ready to serve. Serve the pork with the apple gravy, the vegetables and garnish with thyme sprigs.

Kielbasa
with Sauerkraut and Apples

Here's a super easy meal that can be eaten on its own or made into a hearty sandwich on a hoagie roll.

Serves
4 to 6

Cooking Time
10 Minutes

Release Method
Quick-release

1 tablespoon vegetable oil

28 ounces Polish kielbasa,
cut into 5-inch lengths

1 sweet onion, sliced

1 tablespoon dark brown sugar

1 (2-pound) bag sauerkraut, undrained

1 red apple, Roma or Gala,
peeled and cut into large dice

¼ cup dried currants

½ teaspoon dried thyme

1 (12-ounce) bottle of beer,
preferably a lager

salt and freshly ground black pepper

spicy brown mustard

1. Pre-heat the pressure cooker using the BROWN setting.

2. Heat the oil and brown the kielbasa. Remove the browned sausage and set aside. Add the onion and brown sugar to the cooker and sauté until the onion starts to become tender – about 5 minutes. Add the sauerkraut, apple, dried currants, thyme, and beer to the cooker and stir to combine. Season with salt and freshly ground black pepper. Return the browned kielbasa to the cooker, nestling it into the sauerkraut, onion and apples, and lock the lid in place.

3. Pressure cook on HIGH for 10 minutes.

4. Release the pressure using the QUICK-RELEASE method and carefully remove the lid. Remove the keibasa and sauerkraut with a slotted spoon, draining off much of the liquid. Serve the kielbasa over the bed of sauerkraut with some spicy brown mustard on the side, or make a delicious sandwich on a crusty roll.

Did You Know...?

The sauerkraut sold in bags in the butcher department of your grocery store is crispier than sauerkraut sold in cans and holds up better in this recipe. It's also tastier, in my opinion!

Madeira Ham with Apricots

Cooking a ham in a pressure cooker makes total sense! Most of the hams we buy in the store are already fully cooked. All you need to do to prepare the ham is heat it all the way through without drying it out and add some flavorful glaze. Enter the pressure cooker! Cooking it in the pressure cooker ensures that it will stay moist and you can steam it with any flavors you like. Then, if you want a little color at the end, pop it under the broiler for a few minutes.

Serves
8 to 10

Cooking Time
25 Minutes

Release Method
Natural

1 (5-pound) bone-in ham

12 whole cloves

¼ cup Dijon mustard

¼ - ½ cup brown sugar

1 cup apple juice or cider

1 cup Madeira wine

⅓ cup dried apricots

½ cup raisins

1. Score the ham by making cross hatch slices all over the ham about ¼-inch deep and push the cloves into some of the intersections of the slices. Brush the mustard all over the surface of the ham. Place a rack in the bottom of your pressure cooker and place the ham on top of it. Sprinkle the brown sugar on the ham and pour apple juice and Madeira wine into the cooker. Scatter the apricots and raisins around the side of the ham and lock the lid in place.

2. Pressure cook on HIGH for 25 minutes.

3. Let the pressure drop NATURALLY and carefully remove the lid. Let the ham rest on a cutting board, loosely tented with foil, for at least 10 minutes. In the meantime, turn the cooker to the BROWN setting and reduce the sauce by letting it simmer away while the ham rests. As an option, place the ham under the broiler and brush with some of the sauce to brown the exterior. Serve with a green vegetable and potatoes (the potato gratin on page189 is a great accompaniment).

If you don't have Madeira, you can substitute port, sherry or Marsala wines. If you don't want to use a wine at all, try orange or apple juice or even just some chicken stock.

Pork Chops with Artichokes, Capers, Sundried Tomatoes and Lemons

If you're looking for a boring pork chop, this ain't it! These chops have zing! They are tangy from the lemon and artichokes, salty from the capers and sweet from the tomatoes.

Serves
4

Cooking Time
4 Minutes

Release Method
Natural

2 tablespoons flour

2 teaspoons salt

lots of freshly ground black pepper

4 boneless center cut pork chops, about 1-inch thick

1 tablespoon vegetable oil

2 shallots, finely chopped

1 clove garlic, minced

½ cup dry white wine

1 (15-ounce) can artichoke hearts, halved

¼ cup capers, drained

½ cup sundried tomatoes, julienned

½ cup chicken stock

1 teaspoon Italian seasoning

1 lemon, sliced

1 tablespoon butter, softened

1 tablespoon flour

1 tablespoon chopped fresh parsley

1. Combine flour, salt and pepper. Lightly dredge both sides of the pork chops in the flour, shaking off any excess.

2. Pre-heat the pressure cooker using the BROWN setting.

3. Add the oil to the cooker and brown the pork chops on both sides. Remove the browned chops and set aside. Add the shallots and garlic to the cooker and sauté until the shallots start to brown and soften – about 3 minutes. Add the white wine and stir, scraping up any brown bits on bottom of cooker. Simmer for one minute. Add the artichoke hearts, capers, sundried tomatoes, chicken stock, Italian seasoning and lemon slices. Stir to combine, making sure the lemon slices are submerged in the liquid. Return the pork chops to the cooker and lock the lid in place.

4. Pressure cook on HIGH for 4 minutes.

5. While the pork chops are cooking, mix the butter and flour together in a small bowl to form a paste.

6. Let the pressure drop NATURALLY and carefully remove the lid. Remove pork chops and let them rest for 5 to 10 minutes, loosely covered with foil. Return the cooker to the BROWN setting. Whisk the butter and flour paste into the sauce and bring the liquid to a boil to thicken. Stir in the fresh parsley and season to taste with salt and freshly ground black pepper. Serve the pork chops over rice or angel hair pasta and top with the sauce.

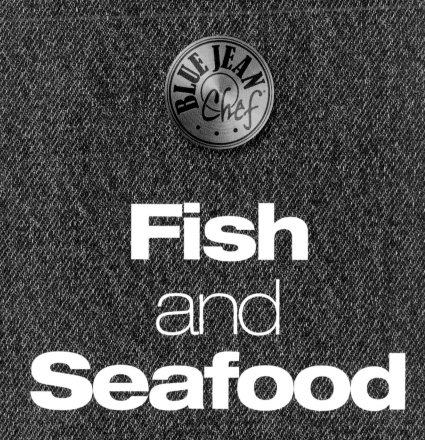

Fish and Seafood

Provençal Fish Stew with Fennel and Potatoes

Calamari Stew

Lime Shrimp and Spicy Tomato Grits

Veracruz Style Snapper with Rice

Salmon Putanesca with White Beans

Thai Coconut Mussels

Provençal Fish Stew
with Fennel and Potatoes

If you like seafood, you'll love this seafood stew. It's not only delicious, but pretty too with all the different types of seafood included. There aren't too many year-round stews, but this is one of them.

Serves
4

Cooking Time
4 Minutes

Release Method
Quick-release

2 tablespoons olive oil

1 onion, finely chopped

1 clove garlic, peeled and smashed

1 teaspoon dried thyme

1 tablespoon tomato paste

2 Yukon Gold potatoes, diced (1-inch)

1 bulb fennel, diced (1-inch)

½ cup dry white wine

1 (28-ounce) can tomatoes, chopped

2 cups seafood stock (or chicken stock if you can't find seafood stock)

1 teaspoon saffron threads (optional)

8 ounces salmon, cut into 1-inch chunks

8 ounces grouper or red snapper, cut into 1-inch chunks

salt and freshly ground black pepper

1 pound mussels (about 20 – 25)

10 medium shrimp, peeled, deveined and tails removed.

3 tablespoons anise-flavored liquor (Pernod, Pastis) (optional)

zest of one orange

¼ cup chopped fresh parsley

1. Pre-heat the pressure cooker using the BROWN setting.

2. Add the olive oil and sauté the onion and garlic until the onion starts to become tender – about 5 minutes. Add the thyme and tomato paste, stir and cook for a minute or two. Add the potatoes, fennel, white wine, tomatoes, stock, saffron (if using) and fish. Stir and season with salt and pepper. Toss the mussels in on top of the stew and lock the lid in place.

3. Cook on HIGH pressure for 4 minutes.

4. Release the pressure using the QUICK-RELEASE method and carefully remove the lid. Immediately add the shrimp to the stew and return the lid to the cooker for three to four minutes. There will be enough residual heat to cook the shrimp, which will change color to bright pink.

5. Stir in the anise-flavored liquor (if using), orange zest and parsley. Remove and discard any mussels whose shells did not open, and serve the stew with a nice chunk of crusty bread to soak up the juices.

Substitution

If you can't find Pernod or Pastis for this recipe, try dry vermouth instead. You might be tempted to try to use Sambuca (another anise or licorice flavored liqueur), but that is a sugar-based liqueur that wouldn't work well with this savory stew.

Calamari Stew

There are two ways to cook calamari – for a very short period of time or for an extended period of time. Anything in between and the squid will be as tough as rubber. The pressure cooker shortens that extended period of time to 20 minutes with a super tender result. When I worked at La Cabro d'Or in the South of France, calamari stew was a regular item on the menu.

Serves
6

Cooking Time
20 Minutes

Release Method
Natural

1 tablespoon olive oil

12 ounces fresh chorizo sausage, casing removed and crumbled (about 3 links)

1 large red onion, sliced

2 cloves garlic, sliced

1 hot chili pepper, de-seeded and sliced

1 pound fresh or frozen squid bodies, cut into 1-inch thick rings

1 teaspoon salt

½ teaspoon dried oregano

½ teaspoon dried thyme

2 tablespoons tomato paste

1 cup dry white wine

2 white potatoes, peeled and diced

1 (28-ounce) can tomatoes, chopped

salt and freshly ground black pepper

½ cup chopped fresh parsley

1. Pre-heat the pressure cooker using the BROWN setting.

2. Add the oil and brown the crumbled chorizo sausage. Add the onion, garlic and chili pepper and sauté for 4 to 5 minutes. Add the squid and season with salt. Cook for a minute and then add the oregano, thyme and tomato paste, and cook for 2 more minutes. Add the white wine and bring to a simmer. Add the potatoes and tomatoes, stir well and lock the lid in place.

3. Pressure cook on HIGH for 20 minutes.

4. Let the pressure drop NATURALLY and carefully remove the lid. Season the sauce to taste with salt and freshly ground black pepper again and stir in the fresh parsley. Spoon the stew out into bowls with crusty bread or serve it ladled over pasta.

Substitution

The Chorizo sausage in this recipe is very important – it's what is going to provide most of the spicy flavor to this stew. So, try to find really good Chorizo sausage. If you can't find really good Chorizo, choose your favorite fresh hot Italian sausage. Whichever sausage you use, make sure it is raw and not a dried or pre-cooked sausage or salami.

Lime Shrimp and Spicy Tomato Grits

Shrimp and grits are often in each other's company, but here the shrimp actually cook in the grits, rather than sitting on top at the end. This is a great marinade for grilled shrimp too.

Serves
4

Cooking Time
10 Minutes

Release Method
Natural

1 pound large shrimp, peeled, deveined and tails removed (about 16 to 20)

¼ cup olive oil

1 clove garlic, sliced

1 tablespoon crushed red pepper flakes

1 tablespoon finely chopped lime zest (about 2 limes)

¼ cup fresh lime juice (about 1½ limes)

2 tablespoons butter

1 Jalapeño pepper, de-seeded and minced

⅛ teaspoon ground cayenne pepper

2 tablespoons tomato paste

4 cups water

1 teaspoon salt

1 cup coarse corn grits (not the instant variety)

2 tomatoes, chopped

chopped fresh chives

1. Start by marinating the shrimp. Combine the olive oil, garlic, crushed red pepper flakes, lime zest and juice in a bowl and toss in shrimp. Set the shrimp aside while you prepare the grits.

2. Pre-heat the pressure cooker using the BROWN setting. Add the butter and Jalapeño pepper and sauté for a couple of minutes. Add the cayenne pepper and tomato paste and stir, cooking for another minute or two. Add the water and salt and bring the mixture to a boil. Whisk the grits into the water, whisking for a full minute so that the grits have a moment to become suspended in the water and not drop to the bottom of the pot. Lock the lid in place.

3. Pressure cook on HIGH for 10 minutes.

4. Let the pressure drop NATURALLY and carefully remove the lid. Give the grits a good stir – they will probably have settled somewhat on the bottom of the cooker. Once you've stirred the grits, immediately remove the shrimp from the marinade with a slotted spoon and stir them into the grits along with the fresh tomatoes. Return the lid to the cooker for 5 minutes. There will be enough residual heat to cook the shrimp through. Season to taste with salt and serve with fresh chives on top.

Did You Know...?

When you are serving shrimp in a dish, think about your guests. When shrimp are stirred right into a dish, remove the tail before you add them to the pot so that your guests don't have embarrassing moments trying to remove the tail themselves.

Veracruz Style Snapper with Rice

Whenever you see "Veracruz" style, think Jalapeño peppers! Veracruz is a Mexican state whose capital is Jalapa (also written Xalapa), which is where Jalapeño peppers were originally cultivated. This is one of my favorite preparations for fish, with both a spicy and a sweet note to it.

Serves
6

Cooking Time
5 Minutes

Release Method
Quick-release

BIG FAV

2 tablespoons olive oil

1 small onion, finely chopped

1 clove garlic, minced

½ teaspoon dried thyme

½ teaspoon dried oregano

1½ cups long-grain white rice

4 tomatoes, diced

½ cup pitted green olives

¼ cup chopped pickled Jalapeño peppers

2 tablespoons capers, rinsed

¼ cup black raisins or currants

¼ cup dry white wine

2 cups chicken stock

6 (7-ounce) fillets of red snapper

salt and freshly ground black pepper

smoked paprika (or regular sweet paprika if you can't find smoked paprika)

¼ cup chopped fresh cilantro (or parsley)

1. Pre-heat the pressure cooker using the BROWN setting.

2. Add the oil and sauté the onion and garlic until the onion starts to become tender – about 5 minutes. Add the thyme and oregano and cook for another minute. Add the rice, tomatoes, olives, pickled Jalapeño peppers, capers, raisins, white wine and chicken stock and stir well. Season with salt and freshly ground black pepper.

3. Season the fish well with salt, pepper and the smoked paprika and nestle the fish into the sauce. Lock the lid in place.

4. Pressure cook on HIGH for 5 minutes.

5. Release the pressure using the QUICK-RELEASE method and carefully remove the lid. Let everything come to an edible temperature and spoon out the rice and fish together, sprinkling cilantro on top.

BLUE JEAN Chef Substitution

If you can't find pickled Jalapeño peppers, try pickled pepperoncini peppers. You might not be able to call it "Veracruz Style", but it will still be delicious!

Fish Facts

One rarely thinks of fish and seafood when it comes to pressure cooking, and frankly that's a shame. It's true that both fish and seafood cook quickly with traditional cooking methods, but there are some advantages to cooking them under pressure. First and foremost, a pressure cooker traps flavor inside the vessel, thereby infusing flavor to what often has a very subtle taste. That means that when you cook fish with flavorful ingredients like wine, coconut milk, juices, herbs or the like, you get that flavor infused into the fish and it remains moist. Of course, fish and seafood also cook in record time in a pressure cooker, but a nice and rarely mentioned bonus is that there is barely any odor in the kitchen when you pressure cook fish – often the main deterrent to cooking fish at home for many people. Finally, it's so easy! If you haven't cooked a lot of fish in the past, now's the time to keep that in the past and embark on your new future with one of the healthiest proteins we can choose. Here are some tips and suggestions for cooking fish under pressure:

■ **Pressure cook fish fillets or steaks that are at least 1-inch thick.**	Any filet of fish will work in a pressure cooker, but I find the best results come from fillets that are about 1-inch thick. Most fish is cooked nicely in 3 to 6 minutes in a pressure cooker, depending on the density of the fillet.
■ **Choose sustainable seafood.**	Not sure which fish are on the danger list? Go to www.seafood-watch.com to find out what the Monterey Bay Aquarium is recommending and which fish they suggest you avoid.
■ **If you're cooking fish by itself in the cooker, protect it from the vigorous boil of the pressure cooker.**	A steamer basket or oven-proof dish on a rack will allow the fish to pressure steam without getting broken apart. Another way to protect the delicate fish fillet is to cook it with other ingredients, like rice or beans, which form a bed on which the fish can lie.
■ **Use the residual high heat from a pressure cooker to cook quick-cooking seafood.**	Shrimp cook very quickly and can be tough if overcooked. I've found the increased temperature of the liquid after the pressure has been released is enough to cook the shrimp as long as you leave it for several minutes. If you're cooking shrimp alone in the pressure cooker, a quick 2 minutes on high pressure will do the job.
■ **Mussels cook really well in the pressure cooker in 4 minutes.**	Clean the mussels by scrubbing them with a brush under running water. Pull off the beard (the whiskery hairs protruding from the shell). It's really important to discard any mussels that are open, broken or don't close their shells when tapped before adding them to your recipe, and any that remain closed after cooking.
■ **Clams are fantastic pressure cooked too, but the cleaning method is a little different to that for mussels.**	Clams on the other hand, should be soaked in cold tap water for about 30 minutes so they spit out any sand that is in their shells. Then, scrub them under running water to remove barnacles or dirt. Always discard any shells that are damaged or open before cooking, and any that remain closed after cooking.

Salmon Putanesca with White Beans

Putanesca is one of my favorite sauces whether it's on pasta or fish. Here, adding white beans to the mix makes this a nice complete meal that just needs a little side salad to go along with it.

Serves
4

Cooking Time
4 + 5 Minutes

Release Method
Combo

1 cup dried white cannellini or navy beans

1 tablespoon olive oil

4 anchovy fillets, chopped (or 2 teaspoons anchovy paste)

1 clove garlic, minced

2 tablespoons capers, rinsed

¾ cup pitted black olives, halved

1 (28-ounce) can tomatoes, chopped

2 tablespoons tomato paste

½ cup dry white wine

½ cup chicken stock

freshly ground black pepper

4 (7-ounce) fillets of salmon

¼ cup chopped fresh parsley

1. Place the beans in the pressure cooker and add water to cover the beans by one inch. Lock the lid in place and pressure cook on HIGH for 4 minutes. Let the pressure drop NATURALLY and carefully remove the lid. Drain the beans and set aside.

2. Pre-heat the pressure cooker using the BROWN setting.

3. Add the oil and sauté the anchovies and garlic for a minute or two, until the anchovies start to melt. Add the capers, black olives, tomatoes, tomato paste, white wine and chicken stock and bring to a simmer. Return the beans to the cooker, season with freshly ground black pepper and nestle the salmon into the sauce. Lock the lid in place.

4. Pressure cook on HIGH for 5 minutes.

5. Release the pressure using the QUICK-RELEASE method and carefully remove the lid. Season to taste with salt (you shouldn't need much if any) and freshly ground black pepper. Transfer the salmon to a platter and spoon the beans and sauce over the top, sprinkling the parsley at the last minute.

Dress It Up

If you want to make this dish really quickly, use two (15-ounce) cans of drained white cannellini beans instead of cooking the beans from scratch. Add the beans just before you add the salmon and keep the cooking time the same.

Thai Coconut Mussels

If you want to make this recipe for 2 people, just reduce the amount of mussels, but keep the steaming liquid quantities the same. Don't forget to put a bowl out for the shells when you serve this!

Serves
4

Cooking Time
4 Minutes

Release Method
Quick-release

4 pounds mussels

1 tablespoon coconut or vegetable oil

2 to 3 shallots (or 1 small onion), sliced

1 clove garlic, sliced

1 inch of fresh gingerroot, peeled and thinly sliced

1 Thai red chili pepper, sliced
(or if you do not want any spice,
use a red bell pepper)

½ cup dry white wine

1 (15-ounce) can unsweetened coconut milk

zest and juice of one lime

¼ cup chopped fresh basil

freshly ground black pepper

1. Clean the mussels by scrubbing them with a brush under running water. Pull off the beard (the whiskery hairs protruding from the shell). Discard any mussels that are open, broken or don't close their shells when tapped.

2. Pre-heat the pressure cooker using the BROWN setting.

3. Add the oil and sauté the shallot, garlic, ginger and red chili pepper for 2 to 3 minutes. Add the wine and coconut milk and stir. Add all the mussels and lock the lid in place.

4. Pressure cook on HIGH for 4 minutes.

5. Release the pressure using the QUICK-RELEASE method and carefully remove the lid. Transfer the mussels to a serving dish, discarding any mussels that did not open (do not force them open). Sprinkle the lime zest and basil on top and squeeze the lime over everything.

Did You Know...?

Lite Coconut milk is really just watered down regular coconut milk. The trouble is that the flavor is really watered down too, so I recommend using the real deal!

Vegetarian Main Dishes

Risotto with Shiitake Mushrooms, Butternut Squash and Peas

Lemon-Basil Ricotta Dumplings

Broccoli Rice Casserole

Miso Brown Rice Bowl with Tofu and Edamame

Spaghetti Squash with Leek and Olive Marinara

Vegetable and Bean Stuffed Peppers with Marinara

Vegetable Couscous with Tomatoes, Feta and Basil

Vegetarian Portobello Mushroom and Zucchini Moussaka

Lentil and Chickpea Stew with Spicy Bitter Greens

Vegetable Coconut Curry

Tadka Dal (Split Red Lentils) with Potatoes

Beetroot Bourguignon with Fingerling Potatoes and Lentils

Risotto with Shiitake Mushrooms, Butternut Squash and Peas

Long gone are the days when making risotto required standing over a stovetop stirring constantly for twenty to thirty minutes. Almost miraculously, a pressure cooker can deliver a risotto in just seven minutes, no stirring required. Using this recipe as a base, you can make any flavored risotto you like.

Serves
6

Cooking Time
7 Minutes

Release Method
Quick-release

1 tablespoon olive oil

1 small onion, finely chopped

3 sprigs fresh thyme

1½ cups ½-inch diced butternut squash

2 cups thinly sliced shiitake mushrooms, stems removed (about 5 ounces)

1½ cups Arborio rice

½ cup white wine

1 cup vegetable stock

2½ cups water

2 teaspoons salt

freshly ground black pepper

½ cup frozen peas, thawed

½ cup grated Parmigiano-Reggiano cheese

1. Pre-heat the pressure cooker using the BROWN setting.

2. Add the oil and cook the onion for a few minutes. Add the thyme, butternut squash and mushrooms and cook for another few minutes. Add the rice, wine, vegetable stock, water, salt and freshly ground black pepper, give everything one good stir and lock the lid in place.

3. Pressure cook on HIGH for 7 minutes.

4. Release the pressure using the QUICK-RELEASE method and carefully remove the lid. Remove the thyme sprigs, stir in the peas and close the lid for 2 minutes to let them warm through. Stir in the cheese and season to taste with salt and freshly ground black pepper.

Did You Know...?

You can use either short-grained Arborio or medium-grained Carnaroli rice for risotto. Carnaroli rice is not as common as Arborio. It has a firmer texture, but still produces a creamy risotto because it has a high starch content.

Lemon-Basil Ricotta Dumplings

Usually a meal involving dumplings is heavy and rich. Not this version, however. These dumplings are made mostly with ricotta cheese (rather than flour), which makes them light in texture, and the lemon adds a nice zip. Serve this with a side salad, and you have a nice dinner for any time of year.

Serves
4

Cooking Time
6 Minutes

Release Method
Natural

1 cup ricotta cheese

½ cup grated Parmesan cheese, plus more for garnish

½ cup shredded fresh basil, plus more for garnish

zest of 1 lemon (about 1 tablespoon)

1 egg, lightly beaten

½ teaspoon salt

freshly ground black pepper

¼ cup all-purpose flour

2 tablespoons olive oil

1 onion, finely chopped

2 cloves garlic, sliced

1 teaspoon dried oregano

2 tablespoons tomato paste

½ cup white wine

2 (28-ounce) cans tomatoes, chopped

1 teaspoon salt

freshly ground black pepper

1. Make the dumplings by combining the ricotta cheese, Parmesan cheese, basil, lemon zest, egg, salt and black pepper in a bowl. Fold in the flour, mixing only to combine - do not over-mix. Set the dumpling mixture aside.

2. Pre-heat the pressure cooker using the BROWN setting.

3. Add the olive oil to the cooker and sauté the onion and garlic until it starts to become tender – about 5 minutes. Add the oregano and tomato paste and stir, cooking for a few more minutes. Pour in the white wine and then add the tomatoes. Season with salt and freshly ground black pepper. Drop dollops of the dumpling mixture into the tomato sauce, letting some of them sink below the surface as necessary, and lock the lid in place.

4. Pressure cook on HIGH for 6 minutes.

5. Let the pressure drop NATURALLY and carefully remove the lid. Let the dumplings and sauce cool to an edible temperature and then serve in bowls with grated Parmesan and fresh basil on top.

Ricotta cheese is an Italian cheese made from whey (the liquid left over when making cheese) and is naturally low in fat, but high in protein. You can make this dish even lower in fat by using the part skim or fat free ricotta versions, although you might find a slight difference in texture.

Broccoli Rice Casserole

You can use fresh OR frozen broccoli florets for this recipe, which makes it a perfect pantry dinner – all the ingredients can be stored in your pantry or freezer, so you'll always be able to make this dish.

Serves
2 to 4

Cooking Time
5 Minutes

Release Method
Quick-release

1 tablespoon vegetable oil

½ onion, finely chopped

pinch crushed red pepper flakes

1 teaspoon dried thyme

1 cup basmati rice

1 cup water

1 (10-ounce) can cream of mushroom soup

2 stalks broccoli, broken into medium sized florets (or 3 cups frozen broccoli florets)

salt, to taste

2 cups grated Cheddar cheese

1. Pre-heat the pressure cooker using the BROWN setting.

2. Add the oil and sauté the onion, red pepper flakes and thyme until the onion starts to soften – about 5 minutes. Add the rice and stir to coat the rice with the oil. Combine the water and mushroom soup, pour the mixture into the cooker and give everything a good stir. Finally, add the broccoli florets, scattering them across the top of the rice. Season with salt and lock the lid in place.

3. Pressure cook on HIGH for 5 minutes.

4. Release the pressure using the QUICK-RELEASE method and carefully remove the lid. Scatter the grated Cheddar cheese on top and return the lid to the cooker for 10 minutes. The rice will continue to steam, the cheese will melt and the casserole will cool to an edible temperature.

You can also add the broccoli stems to this recipe.
Just make sure you dice the stalks into ½-inch dice.

Miso Brown Rice Bowl with Tofu and Edamame

There are so many health benefits to this meal that I don't have room to list them here. But, health benefits are not what make us want to eat dinner. It's the sweet and salty miso sauce flavor that really makes this a rice bowl you'll want to come back to again and again. I have to give recipe credit here to my friend, Lynn who is an excellent cook and brought great flavors to the table with this recipe.

Serves
6 to 8

Cooking Time
20 Minutes

Release Method
Natural

¼ cup light miso paste

¼ cup soy sauce

2 tablespoons minced fresh ginger (peeled)

2 cloves garlic, minced

⅛ teaspoon ground cayenne

4 teaspoons rice vinegar

¼ cup mirin (Japanese sweet rice wine)

2 tablespoons honey

1 tablespoon toasted sesame seeds

3 scallions, thinly sliced (white and light green parts only)

1 pound extra firm tofu, drained and cut into small cubes

1½ cups brown rice

1 red bell pepper, finely chopped

1 carrot, peeled and grated

1½ cups vegetable broth

1 (8-ounce) bag frozen edamame (soy beans), defrosted

1. To make the miso sauce, mix together the first ten ingredients in a bowl and stir well.

2. In a separate bowl, toss the tofu with ¼ cup of the miso sauce. Set aside.

3. Place the brown rice, red pepper, carrot, vegetable broth and ¼ cup of the miso sauce into the pressure cooker. Lock the lid in place.

4. Pressure cook on HIGH for 20 minutes.

5. Let the pressure drop NATURALLY and carefully remove the lid.

6. Fold the tofu and edamame into the rice. Return the lid to the cooker and let the mixture sit for a minute or two to warm the tofu and edamame. Serve with the remaining sauce at the table.

Miso is a Japanese seasoning paste made from fermented soybeans. While that might not sound very appetizing, it's a delicious salty seasoning with health benefits to boot! Miso is a complete protein that aids in digestion, boosts the immune system and can lower bad cholesterol. You will find miso in a tub, refrigerated, often near the produce section with other refrigerated dressings.

If you can't find mirin – a sweet Japanese cooking wine – then you can substitute dry sherry, sweet marsala or white wine with a good pinch of sugar.

Spaghetti Squash
with Leek and Olive Marinara

Few meals leave me feeling as fresh and healthy as a bowl of spaghetti squash with marinara sauce. Cooking the squash in the pressure cooker saves so much time and is easy and tidy. While the squash cools, there's just enough time to make a delicious marinara to go over the top. Remember to top it all with true Parmigiano-Reggiano cheese – there is no substitute!

Serves
4 to 6

Cooking Time
15 + 5 Minutes

Release Method
Quick-release

1 spaghetti squash, halved and seeds removed

salt and freshly ground black pepper

2 tablespoons olive oil

2 leeks, cleaned and sliced 1-inch thick (about 3 cups)

3 cloves garlic, finely chopped

¼ teaspoon crushed red pepper flakes

1 teaspoon dried oregano

¾ cup pitted black olives, halved

1 (28-ounce) can tomatoes, chopped

1 (28-ounce) can tomatoes, crushed

2 tablespoons tomato paste

½ cup water

½ cup grated Parmigiano-Reggiano cheese

¼ cup chopped fresh parsley

1. Season the cut side of the spaghetti squash with salt and pepper. Place the spaghetti squash halves, cut side down on a rack in the pressure cooker. (It's alright if they are stacked on top of each other.) Add 2 cups of water to the cooker and lock the lid in place.

2. Pressure cook on HIGH for 15 minutes (depending on the size of the spaghetti squash).

3. Release the pressure using the QUICK-RELEASE method and carefully remove the lid. Remove the spaghetti squash halves from the cooker using tongs and set aside to cool.

4. While the spaghetti squash cools, make the marinara. Empty and clean the pressure cooker insert. Pre-heat the pressure cooker using the BROWN setting. Add the olive oil and sauté the leeks until they start to turn brown on the edges – about 4 minutes. Add the garlic, crushed red pepper flakes, oregano and olives and cook for another minute or two. Add the tomatoes, tomato paste and water, season with salt and lock the lid in place.

5. Pressure cook on HIGH for 5 minutes.

6. Release the pressure using the QUICK-RELEASE method and carefully remove the lid. When the spaghetti squash is cool enough to handle, scrape the squash with a fork, pulling the strands of squash away from the skin. Season the strands of squash with salt and freshly ground black pepper to taste and then top with the marinara. Sprinkle the Parmigiano-Reggiano cheese and parsley on top just before serving.

If you're really in a hurry, you can start the marinara sauce in a sauté pan on the stovetop while the spaghetti squash is cooking in the pressure cooker. Once all the ingredients are in the pan, remove the pan from the heat. As soon as the spaghetti squash has finished cooking, add the sauce ingredients to the pressure cooker, lock the lid in place and cook. In the quick five minutes it takes for the spaghetti squash to cool, the sauce will be done.

Vegetable and Bean Stuffed Peppers with Marinara

Here's a meal that is super quick and easy to throw together. It can be spicy or mild, depending on what salsa you use, so pick your favorite. Served with rice and a green salad, it's a bright and colorful meal.

Serves
4

Cooking Time
12 Minutes

Release Method
Quick-release

4 large bell peppers (red, green, yellow or orange)

¾ cup frozen peas

¾ cup frozen corn

1 (15-ounce) can kidney beans or chickpeas, drained and rinsed

1 cup grated Cheddar cheese

½ cup salsa

¼ cup chopped fresh parsley or cilantro

1 teaspoon salt

freshly ground black pepper

1 cup vegetable stock

1 cup marinara sauce

1. Slice off the tops of the peppers and hollow out the insides, removing the seeds and veins. Slice a tiny slice off the bottom of the pepper to ensure that it sits flat, but don't cut through the pepper.

2. Combine the peas, corn, beans, cheese, salsa, parsley or cilantro, salt and pepper in a bowl. Gently spoon this mixture into the peppers.

3. Place a rack into the pressure cooker and pour the vegetable stock into the cooker. Place the stuffed peppers on top of the rack, resting them against the sides of the cooker and each other to keep them standing upright. Spoon ¼ cup of marinara on each pepper and lock the lid in place.

4. Pressure cook on HIGH for 12 minutes.

5. Release the pressure using the QUICK-RELEASE method and carefully remove the lid. Let the peppers rest in the cooker until they are an edible temperature. Use tongs and a spoon to transfer the peppers from the cooker to a plate and serve with white rice or a green salad.

Did You Know...?

Cilantro looks a lot like parsley. If you can't recognize the difference between the two visually, the best way to tell them apart is to taste a little leaf. Cilantro has more curved leaves and a prominent taste. You can store cilantro for up to a week in the refrigerator if you place the stems in a glass of water and cover the top with a plastic bag.

Vegetable Couscous
with Tomatoes, Feta and Basil

This is a great dish full of vegetables to serve warm or at room temperature for spring or summer. Be sure to use a high-quality extra virgin olive oil here for the best flavor along with lots of fresh herbs.

Serves
6 to 8

Cooking Time
3 Minutes

Release Method
Quick-release

2 tablespoons olive oil

1 onion, finely chopped

1 clove garlic, smashed

1 red pepper, diced ¾-inch

1 yellow pepper, diced ¾-inch

1 zucchini, diced ¾-inch

1 yellow squash, diced ¾-inch

2 cups small broccoli florets

12 stalks of asparagus, sliced ½-inch thick on the bias

salt and freshly ground black pepper

2 cups vegetable stock

2 cups whole-grain couscous (or regular couscous)

1½ cups halved cherry tomatoes

1½ cups crumbled feta cheese

2 tablespoons chopped fresh chives

½ cup shredded fresh basil

1 lemon, to juice

extra virgin olive oil

1. Pre-heat the pressure cooker using the BROWN setting.

2. Add the olive oil and sauté the onion and garlic for 5 minutes. Add the peppers, zucchini, squash, broccoli florets and asparagus, and stir well. Season with salt and freshly ground black pepper and add the vegetable stock. Lock the lid in place.

3. Pressure cook on HIGH for 3 minutes.

4. Release the pressure using the QUICK-RELEASE method and carefully remove the lid. Immediately stir in the couscous and return the lid to the cooker for 5 minutes.

5. Fluff the couscous with a fork as you transfer everything to a large serving or salad bowl. Toss in the cherry tomatoes, feta cheese and herbs. Season to taste with salt, freshly ground black pepper, a squeeze of fresh lemon juice and extra virgin olive oil. Serve warm at room temperature.

If you really want dinner in a hurry, use the pre-cut vegetables that you find in the grocery store produce section. As long as they are roughly the same size, they will be fine. If they are bigger than 1-inch dice, add a minute to the cooking time.

Portobello Mushroom and Zucchini Moussaka

This recipe uses the pressure cooker to speed up the making of moussaka, but ultimately the casserole still gets baked in an oven. This recipe was just too good not to include in the book, and making it faster to prepare earns it a page!

Serves
6 to 8

Cooking Time
4 + 5 Minutes
+ 35 minutes
in the oven

Release Method
Quick-release

1 large eggplant (or 2 medium eggplants)

2 tablespoons olive oil

1 onion, finely diced

2 carrots, finely diced

2 ribs celery, finely diced

2 cloves garlic, minced

12 ounces Portobello (or Baby Bella) mushrooms, diced into ½-inch chunks

1 large zucchini, diced into ½-inch chunks

1 teaspoon dried oregano

1 teaspoon ground cinnamon

1 teaspoon salt

¼ teaspoon crushed red pepper flakes

½ cup white wine

½ cup vegetable stock

1 (28-ounce) can crushed tomatoes

2 cups Greek yogurt

1 cup grated Parmesan cheese

¼ teaspoon ground nutmeg

1 egg, lightly beaten

salt and pepper, to taste

2 tablespoons instant potato flakes

½ cup crumbled Feta cheese

1. Cut the eggplant in half lengthwise and place the halves on a rack in the pressure cooker cut side up. (It's ok if they stack or rest on top of each other.) Add 1 cup of water, season the eggplant with salt and lock the lid in place.

2. Pressure cook on HIGH for 4 minutes.

3. Release the pressure using the QUICK-RELEASE method and carefully remove the lid. Transfer the eggplant to a resting plate, and when cool enough to handle, slice each half into half moons, about ¾-inch thick. Place the eggplant slices in a single layer on the bottom of a 12-inch oven-safe casserole dish.

4. Pre-heat the pressure cooker using the BROWN setting.

5. Add the oil and sauté the onion, carrots, celery and garlic until the vegetables start to become tender – about 5 minutes. Add the mushrooms, zucchini and spices and stir well. Add the wine, stock and tomatoes and lock the lid in place.

6. Pressure cook on HIGH for 5 minutes.

7. While the sauce is cooking, combine the Greek yogurt, Parmesan cheese, nutmeg and egg in a bowl, blend well and set aside. Pre-heat the oven to 400° F.

8. Release the pressure using the QUICK-RELEASE method and carefully remove the lid. Stir the potato flakes into the pressure cooker (these will help thicken the sauce) and season to taste with salt and freshly ground black pepper. Transfer the sauce to the casserole dish, creating a layer on top of the eggplant slices. Dollop the yogurt-cheese mixture on top of the casserole and do your best to smooth it out. Transfer the casserole dish to the oven for 35 to 40 minutes, or until the top is golden brown. Let the moussaka cool before serving with the Feta cheese sprinkled on top.

Greek yogurt is not known as "Greek yogurt" in Greece? There, they just call it "strained yogurt" or straggisto. Regardless of what you call it, Greek yogurt is yogurt that has been strained to remove the whey, lactose and sugar.

Lentil and Chickpea Stew with Spicy Bitter Greens

This is a hearty winter stew that will warm you up and keep you satiated for a long time. There are lots of ways to vary this stew from batch to batch by swapping out different greens - try chard, beet greens, dandelion greens or even turnip greens for a change of pace.

Serves
4

Cooking Time
7 Minutes

Release Method
Quick-release

2 tablespoons olive oil

1 onion, finely chopped

2 carrots, sliced

2 ribs celery, sliced

2 cloves garlic, smashed

½ teaspoon ground cumin

1 teaspoon dried thyme

½ teaspoon crushed red pepper flakes

1 cup brown or green lentils

1 (15-ounce) can chickpeas, drained and rinsed

1 (28-ounce) can tomatoes, chopped

4 cups vegetable stock

2 cups water

salt and freshly ground black pepper

2 cups fresh bitter greens, shredded (i.e. kale, chard, spinach, beet greens, mustard greens, turnip greens)

1 lemon, to juice

1. Pre-heat the pressure cooker using the BROWN setting.

2. Add the olive oil and sauté the onion, carrots and celery for 5 to 6 minutes. Add the garlic and spices and cook for another minute or two. Stir in the lentils, chickpeas, tomatoes, stock and water, and season with salt and freshly ground black pepper. Lock the lid in place.

3. Pressure cook on HIGH for 7 minutes.

4. Release the pressure using the QUICK-RELEASE method and carefully remove the lid. Stir in the bitter greens and let them sit in the stew to wilt while the stew comes to an edible temperature. Season again to taste with salt, pepper and a squeeze of lemon juice. Serve with a big piece of crusty bread.

BLUE JEAN Chef

Did You Know...?

Bitter greens are members of the lettuce family that tend to be dark in color, are full of nutrients and vitamins, and are generally enjoyed cooked rather than raw (although arugula is a well-known exception). Kale is the leading lady of the bitter green family these days, but there are a lot of different varieties that would work well in this stew.

Vegetable Coconut Curry

The coconut flavor in this curry comes in the form of coconut cream at the end of cooking. Coconut cream is the thick milky substance that rises to the surface in a can of whole coconut milk, so don't try to substitute light coconut milk for this recipe.

Serves
4 to 6

Cooking Time
6 Minutes

Release Method
Quick-release

1 tablespoon vegetable oil (or coconut oil)

1 onion, chopped into large chunks

2 carrots, sliced

1 yellow pepper, chopped into large chunks

1 red chili, sliced (optional)

2 cloves garlic, minced

1 tablespoon grated fresh gingerroot

2 tablespoons really good curry powder

1½ cups vegetable stock

2 tomatoes, chopped or ½ pint cherry tomatoes

2 white potatoes, scrubbed and cut into large chunks

1 cup small cauliflower florets

1 cup small broccoli florets

salt and freshly ground black pepper

the coconut cream from 1 (14-ounce) can coconut milk

2 cups fresh spinach leaves

¼ cup fresh cilantro or basil, for garnish

½ cup chopped cashews

1 lime, cut into wedges

1. Pre-heat the pressure cooker using the BROWN setting.

2. Add the oil to the pressure cooker and sauté the onion, carrots, yellow pepper and red chili (if using) for about 5 minutes. Add the garlic, ginger and curry powder and cook for another minute. Add the stock, tomatoes, potatoes, cauliflower and broccoli florets, and stir to combine well. Season with salt and freshly ground black pepper and lock the lid in place.

3. Cook on HIGH pressure for 6 minutes.

4. Release the pressure using the QUICK-RELEASE method and carefully remove the lid. Add the coconut cream to the cooker while the curry is still hot, stirring to combine well. Stir in the spinach and let it wilt while the curry comes to an edible temperature. Season to taste with salt and pepper and serve with the cilantro or basil leaves, the chopped cashews and a wedge of lime for squeezing.

Did You Know...?

The easiest way to make sure the coconut cream rises to the surface of a can of coconut milk is to keep the can in the refrigerator before you use it. If it's cold, you'll be able to open up the can and spoon the cream right off the top. Make sure to lick the spoon – it's delicious!

Tadka Dal (Split Red Lentils) with Potatoes

Tadka translates as "tempering" which is what happens at the end of this recipe – you temper the lentils with a spicy mixture sautéed on the stovetop in butter. This is where you can really add some heat to the dish with a spicy red chili, or take it easy with a more gentle pepper like a Jalapeño.

Serves
4 to 6

Cooking Time
7 Minutes

Release Method
Quick-release

1 tablespoon vegetable oil

1 onion, finely chopped

1 clove garlic, minced

2 teaspoons grated fresh ginger

1 Jalapeño pepper, sliced into rings
(with or without seeds)

2 cups red lentils, rinsed

2 cups diced, peeled white potato
(about 2 medium potatoes diced ¾-inch)

½ teaspoon ground turmeric

1 teaspoon salt

5 cups water or vegetable stock

3 tablespoons ghee or clarified butter
(see note)

1 red chili pepper, sliced into rings
(or another Jalapeño pepper)

1 teaspoon brown mustard seeds

1 teaspoon cumin seeds

2 teaspoons sesame seeds

2 tomatoes, chopped

½ teaspoon garam masala
(or ½ teaspoon ground cumin and
a pinch of ground allspice)

salt

fresh cilantro leaves (optional)

1. Pre-heat the pressure cooker using the BROWN setting.

2. Add the oil and sauté the onion until it starts to become tender – about 5 minutes. Add the garlic, ginger and Jalapeño pepper and stir for a minute or two. Add the lentils, potatoes, turmeric and salt, and pour in the water or vegetable stock. Give everything a good stir and lock the lid in place.

3. Pressure cook on HIGH for 7 minutes.

4. While the dal is cooking, pre-heat a skillet over medium-high heat. Add the ghee or clarified butter and when it is very hot, add the red chili pepper, mustard, cumin and sesame seeds. The seeds may pop and sizzle. When the pepper is just starting to brown and the seeds are very fragrant, add the tomatoes and cook until the tomato starts to melt a little – about 2 minutes. Add the garam masala and set aside.

5. Release the pressure using the QUICK-RELEASE method and carefully remove the lid. Check the consistency of the dal, adding a little more liquid if necessary. It should be swirl-able in the pot and not too thick. Season to taste with salt. Serve in bowls with some of the hot tomato mixture on top and a leaf or two of cilantro. This is nice with a bowl of rice or some Indian naan bread.

You can buy clarified butter, or make your own. Melt a stick of butter on the stovetop on medium heat. It should boil and bubble and make noise while the water evaporates. When the noise stops, you'll be left with just butter fat and milk solids. The milk solids will either fall to the bottom of the pot and start to brown, or rise to the surface as white foam. Take the pot off the heat, scoop the foam from the top and pour the clarified butter through a piece of cheesecloth or a fine strainer. Store in the fridge for a couple of months.

Beetroot Bourguignon
with Fingerling Potatoes and Lentils

This recipe was inspired by the Beet Bourguignon recipe on one of my favorite food blogs, Green Kitchen Stories. This is an earthy stew of vegetables and lentils cooked in a red wine broth. I like to top it with a little dollop of sour cream and horseradish mixed together.

Serves
6 to 8

Cooking Time
18 Minutes

Release Method
Quick-release

2 tablespoons olive oil

1 (6-ounce) bag pearl onions (or frozen pearl onions, thawed and dried)

2 cloves garlic, smashed

5 medium carrots, cut into 3-inch lengths

½ teaspoon dried oregano

¼ teaspoon dried rosemary

5 sprigs fresh thyme

½ cup French green lentils

6 beets, peeled and cut into wedges

6 small crimini mushrooms, left whole or halved

8 fingerling potatoes, cut in half if they are large

salt and freshly ground black pepper

2 cups red wine

3 cups vegetable stock

2 tablespoons flour

1 tablespoon butter, softened to room temperature

¼ cup chopped fresh parsley

1. Pre-heat the pressure cooker using the BROWN setting.

2. Add the olive oil to the cooker and sauté the pearl onions until they just start to get a little color – about 6 to 8 minutes. Add the garlic, carrots and spices, and cook for another 3 minutes or so. Add the lentils, beets, mushrooms and potatoes and season with salt and pepper. Add the wine and vegetable stock and lock the lid in place.

3. Pressure cook on HIGH for 18 minutes.

4. While the vegetables are cooking, combine the flour and butter in a small bowl to form a paste, called a beurre manié.

5. Release the pressure using the QUICK-RELEASE method and carefully remove the lid. Transfer the vegetables and lentils to a serving bowl with a slotted spoon. Return the pressure cooker to the BROWN setting and bring the braising liquid to a boil. Whisk the beurre manié into the braising liquid to thicken slightly. Pour the sauce over the vegetables and sprinkle the parsley on top.

Dress It Up

Combine ½ cup of sour cream with 2 tablespoons of prepared horseradish in a small bowl. Season with a pinch of salt and some freshly ground black pepper. Dollop this on top of each bowl just before serving.

Grains and Beans

Farro Salad with Hazelnuts, Arugula, Grapes

Hoppin' John (or Black-Eyed Peas with Rice)

Quinoa Rice with Almonds

Mexican Brown Rice with Corn and Chilies

Saffron Rice with Chickpeas

Smoky Bacon Tomato Chickpeas

Quinoa and Lentils with Mango and Mint

Brown Rice Salad with Artichoke Hearts, Avocado and Pinenuts

Farro Salad
with Hazelnuts, Arugula and Grapes

Farro was the primary grain in Ancient Rome and some consider it to be the "original wheat species". It's easy to cook, has a delicious nutty flavor, is high in fiber and is a good source of protein and iron. What's better than easy, healthy AND delicious?

Serves
4

Cooking Time
18 Minutes

Release Method
Quick-release

1 cup farro

3 cups water

pinch of salt

2 cups arugula

½ cup toasted hazelnuts

1 cup seedless red grapes, halved

2 teaspoons orange zest

¼ cup fresh parsley leaves,
rough chopped

¼ cup fresh mint leaves, rough chopped

2 teaspoons white balsamic vinegar

2 tablespoons extra virgin olive oil

salt and freshly ground black pepper,
to taste

1. Place the farro and water in the pressure cooker, along with a good pinch of salt and lock the lid in place.

2. Pressure cook on HIGH for 18 minutes.

3. While the farro is cooking, prepare the remaining ingredients by combining the arugula, hazelnuts, grapes, orange zest and herbs in a large bowl. In a separate small bowl, whisk the white balsamic vinegar, extra virgin olive oil, salt and freshly ground black pepper together and set aside.

4. Release the pressure using the QUICK-RELEASE method and carefully remove the lid. Strain the farro, discarding any excess liquid, and spread it out onto a cookie sheet to let it cool for about 10 minutes. Then, add the farro to the bowl with the remaining ingredients and toss everything together with the vinaigrette. Serve at room temperature.

This salad is also delicious with fresh pomegranate. The tidiest way to get pomegranate seeds (called arils) out of the pomegranate is to cut the pomegranate in quarters and then submerge each piece in a bowl of water while you pick out the seeds with your fingers. The bitter white pith will rise to the surface of the water. Scoop that up with your hands and discard. Strain off the water and you'll be left with just the seeds…or arils.

Spill the Beans

A pressure cooker is a great way to venture into the world of grains and beans, and work new dishes into your cooking repertoire. For most of us leading busy lives, cooking beans from their dried state just takes up too much time. With a pressure cooker, however, you really can find the time to make homemade beans for any dish, and they taste so much better than their canned counterparts. Rice and other grains are also perfectly cooked in a pressure cooker in a fraction of the time it usually takes on the stovetop. Here are some tips to get you into that exciting world of beans and grains.

To soak or not to soak?

Although you don't have to soak beans ahead of time, they cook faster and taste better if they have been soaked. In addition, soaking beans and discarding the soaking water can help with the flatulent affect that beans have on all of us, which in my opinion is reason enough! The traditional method of soaking beans is to cover them abundantly with water and leave them on the counter for 8 to 12 hours. If you are not a good planner and have forgotten to soak your beans, you can do a "quick soak" method in the pressure cooker. Cover them with at least one inch of water and pressure cook on HIGH for 2 to 4 minutes, depending on how long they will cook in the subsequent recipe. Let the pressure drop naturally, drain away the water, rinse the beans and then use them as intended.

Let them down naturally.

Beans need a natural release for two reasons. First of all, a quick-release can often cause the skins of the beans to burst open. Secondly, a quick-release can cause the bean liquid to sputter out of the release valve, making a mess. Natural release methods can take as long as fifteen minutes, but it's important.

Half full or half empty?

Regardless of your outlook, don't fill the pressure cooker above the halfway mark when you're cooking beans or grains. Both expand and need that extra room in the cooker in order to do so.

The right time to season.

Don't add salt to beans when you are quick-soaking them. Salt will prolong the cooking time. It's better to add salt to beans at the end when all the other ingredients have been mixed in. Grains, on the other hand, do taste better if you season them while they are cooking, so add salt at the beginning.

Oil if alone.

If you're cooking beans or grains by themselves, add a little fat (butter or oil) to help minimize the foaming inside the cooker.

Pay attention to ratios.

Very little if any evaporation occurs in a pressure cooker, so the ratios of grains to liquid are different for pressure-cooking than for traditional methods. You'll see those ratios on the time chart for grains and beans on page 240 and it's important to follow them.

Hoppin' John (or Black-Eyed Peas w/ Rice)

Hoppin' John is a dish made with rice and peas served in the southern United States. Eating Hoppin' John on New Year's Day along with some collard greens is supposed to bring you luck and prosperity. With luck and prosperity on the line, use the best rice that you can get your hands on. If you can manage to get some true Carolina Gold rice, I think you'll feel lucky just enjoying the Hoppin' John!

Serves
6 to 8

Cooking Time
2 + 6 Minutes

Release Method
Combo

2 cups dried black-eyed peas

2 slices bacon, chopped

1 onion, finely chopped

2 green bell peppers, finely chopped

3 cloves garlic, minced

2 cups long-grain rice

7 ounces ham, diced into ½-inch chunks

1 teaspoon dried thyme

½ teaspoon crushed red pepper flakes

3½ cups chicken stock

2 teaspoons salt

3 cups shredded collard greens

freshly ground black pepper

2 tablespoons cider vinegar

3 scallions, chopped

1. Place the black-eyed peas in the pressure cooker and cover with an inch of water. Pressure cook on HIGH for 2 minutes. Let the pressure drop NATURALLY and carefully remove the lid. Drain and set the peas aside.

2. Heat the pressure cooker using the BROWN setting.

3. Add the bacon and sauté until the bacon is crispy. Remove the bacon with a slotted spoon and set aside. Add the onion, green pepper and garlic to the cooker and sauté until they start to become tender – about 5 minutes. Add the rice, ham and spices and continue to cook for another two minutes. Return the peas to the cooker, along with the chicken stock, salt and collard greens. Stir and lock the lid in place.

4. Pressure cook on HIGH for 6 minutes.

5. Release the pressure using the QUICK-RELEASE method and carefully remove the lid. Give the peas and rice a gentle stir, mixing in the reserved bacon and the cider vinegar. Season to taste with salt and freshly ground black pepper, moisten with more chicken stock if desired, and sprinkle the scallions on top at the end.

Shortcut

You can make this lucky dish in just 6 minutes if you use canned black-eyed peas. Just skip step 1 and add the peas where you would normally return the par-cooked beans to the cooker.

Quinoa Rice
with Almonds

Quinoa is actually a seed, rather than a grain. The great thing about quinoa is that it is super high in protein and fits into a gluten-free diet really well. You can use red or white quinoa in this dish, depending on the look you want at the end. I think the red quinoa is particularly pretty.

Serves
4

Cooking Time
HIGH 6 Minutes

Release Method
Natural

2 tablespoons butter, divided

½ onion, finely chopped

1 clove garlic, smashed

1 cup basmati rice

½ cup quinoa, rinsed

2 teaspoons salt

freshly ground black pepper

2½ cups water

½ cup chopped toasted almonds

1. Pre-heat the pressure cooker using the BROWN setting.

2. Add 1 tablespoon of the butter and cook the onion and garlic until the onion starts to become tender – about 5 minutes. Stir in the rice, quinoa, salt and pepper. Add the water and lock the lid in place.

3. Pressure cook on HIGH for 6 minutes.

4. Let the pressure drop NATURALLY and carefully remove the lid. Fluff the rice with a fork, remove the garlic clove, stir in the remaining butter and toasted almonds and serve.

The butter in this recipe is there purely for flavor, so if you're trying to lighten up, just leave out the butter and consider a little drizzle of olive oil at the end.

Mexican Brown Rice with Corn and Chilies

Brown rice has a nice nuttiness and is a little chewier than white rice. Mixing it up with the corn, chilies and tomatoes makes it a tasty accompaniment or even a meal unto itself!

Serves
6

Cooking Time
20 Minutes

Release Method
Natural

1 tablespoon olive oil

1 onion, finely chopped

1 Poblano pepper (or green bell pepper), chopped

1 teaspoon dried oregano

1 tablespoon chili powder

⅛ teaspoon ground cayenne pepper

2 tomatoes, chopped

½ cup pickled Jalapeño peppers, drained

2 cups brown rice

2 teaspoons salt

freshly ground black pepper

4 cups water or chicken stock

1 cup fresh (or frozen and thawed) corn kernels

¼ cup fresh cilantro leaves

1 cup fresh cherry tomatoes, halved

1. Pre-heat the pressure cooker using the BROWN setting.

2. Add the oil and sauté the onion until it starts to become tender – about 5 minutes. Add the Poblano pepper, oregano, chili powder, and cayenne pepper and cook for another minute. Stir in the tomatoes, Jalapeño peppers, rice, salt and freshly ground black pepper. Add the water or chicken stock and lock the lid in place.

3. Pressure cook on HIGH for 20 minutes.

4. Let the pressure drop NATURALLY and carefully remove the lid. Add the corn kernels and fluff them into the rice with a fork. Let the corn kernels heat through and then serve the rice with the cilantro and cherry tomatoes on top.

Did You Know...?

Brown rice is simply whole grain rice that has only the hull removed, leaving the bran and germ (the most nutritious part of the grain) intact. The deterrent to cooking brown rice is that it usually takes about 40 minutes on the stovetop. The pressure cooker cuts that time in half. Getting healthy in half the time? I wish that applied to my time at the gym!

Saffron Rice
with Chickpeas

I love chickpeas (also called Garbanzo beans)! I also love mixing beans and rice together. Throw some saffron in the mix, making them a pretty yellow color and I'm a happy cook!

Serves
4

Cooking Time
5 + 6 Minutes

Release Method
Combo

¾ cup dried chickpeas

1 tablespoon vegetable oil

1 tablespoon butter

½ onion, finely chopped

2 cloves garlic, sliced

1 teaspoon saffron threads

1 cup basmati rice

1¾ cups water

1½ teaspoons salt

freshly ground black pepper

¼ cup chopped fresh cilantro or parsley

1. Place the chickpeas in the pressure cooker and cover with an inch of water. Pressure cook on HIGH for 5 minutes. Let the pressure drop NATURALLY for 15 minutes. Release any residual pressure with the QUICK-RELEASE method and carefully remove the lid. Drain and set the chickpeas aside.

2. Pre-heat the pressure cooker using the BROWN setting.

3. Add the oil and butter and cook the onion, garlic and saffron threads until the onion starts to become tender – about 5 minutes. Add the rice and stir well. Return the chickpeas to the cooker, pour in the water, season with the salt and pepper and lock the lid in place.

4. Pressure cook on HIGH for 6 minutes.

5. Reduce the pressure using the QUICK-RELEASE method and carefully remove the lid. Fluff the rice and chickpeas with a fork, mixing in the cilantro or parsley and transfer to a serving dish.

Though I think cooking your chickpeas from their dried form is so much tastier, if you're in a hurry, use a can of chickpeas in this recipe. Drain and rinse the chickpeas and then add them to the cooker and cook them with the rice.

Smoky Bacon Tomato Chickpeas

The first time I ever had chickpeas in a smoky tomato sauce was at one of my favorite restaurants in Philadelphia – José Garces' flagship restaurant, Amada. I could eat a bowl of these for dinner, but they make a great side dish too.

Serves
4 to 6

Cooking Time
8 + 10 Minutes

Release Method
Combo

2 cups dried chickpeas

4 ounces thick sliced bacon, chopped (about 4 slices)

2 cloves garlic, sliced

1 teaspoon smoked paprika

1 (28-ounce) can fire roasted tomatoes, chopped

½ cup water

1½ teaspoons salt

freshly ground black pepper

1. Place the chickpeas in the pressure cooker and cover with an inch of water. Pressure cook on HIGH for 8 minutes. Let the pressure drop NATURALLY for 15 minutes. Release any residual pressure using the QUICK-RELEASE method and carefully remove the lid. Drain and set the chickpeas aside.

2. Heat the pressure cooker using the BROWN setting.

3. Add the bacon and cook until crispy. Remove the bacon with a slotted spoon and set aside. Drain off all but 1 tablespoon of the bacon fat and add the garlic to the cooker, sautéing for just a minute. Return the chickpeas to the cooker and add the smoked paprika. Stir and cook for another minute. Add the tomatoes and water and lock the lid in place.

4. Pressure cook on HIGH for 10 minutes.

5. While the chickpeas are cooking, chop the bacon into finely chopped pieces.

6. Release the pressure using the QUICK-RELEASE method and carefully remove the lid. Let the chickpeas cool to an edible temperature and season to taste with salt and freshly ground black pepper. Serve with crumbled bacon on top.

 Did You Know....?

The older chickpeas get, the longer they take to cook and soften. Try buying your chickpeas from a bulk bin and only buy what you need so that the chickpeas in your house never get old.

Quinoa and Lentils
with Mango and Mint

Protein and Protein!! With both quinoa and lentils, you'd think this could be a heavy dish, but the mango and mint give it a sweet, bright note that will keep you going back for more and feeling full for a while.

Serves
4

Cooking Time
7 Minutes

Release Method
Quick-release

1 cup Du Puy lentils
(dark green French lentils)

1 cup quinoa

2 teaspoons salt

3 cups water

1 mango, peeled and diced

½ cup chopped fresh mint leaves

2 to 3 tablespoons extra virgin olive oil

1 tablespoon white balsamic vinegar

salt and freshly ground black pepper

1. Combine the lentils, quinoa, salt and water in the pressure cooker and lock the lid in place.

2. Pressure cook on HIGH for 7 minutes.

3. Release the pressure using the QUICK-RELEASE method and carefully remove the lid. Strain the quinoa and lentils and let them cool by spreading them out on a cookie sheet for about 5 minutes. Then, toss the quinoa and lentils with the mango, mint, olive oil and vinegar. Season to taste with salt and freshly ground black pepper and serve.

If you can't find white balsamic vinegar, you can use regular balsamic vinegar, but just expect the dish to be a darker color.

Brown Rice Salad with Artichoke Hearts, Avocado and Pinenuts

This is another room temperature salad, which means that you can make it ahead of time and focus on the main meal at hand. Or, this could actually be a main course salad all by itself.

Serves
8 (or 4 people as a main meal)

Cooking Time
20 Minutes

Release Method
Natural

1 tablespoon olive oil

1 onion, finely chopped

2 cups brown rice

2 teaspoons salt

freshly ground black pepper

4 cups water or chicken stock

1 tablespoon rice wine vinegar

½ teaspoon honey

½ teaspoon salt

freshly ground black pepper

3 tablespoons extra virgin olive oil

1 (12-ounce) jar artichoke hearts in water, drained and quartered

1 avocado, diced

2 ribs celery, thinly sliced

6 radishes, sliced

1½ cups halved cherry tomatoes

⅓ cup toasted pinenuts

¾ cup fresh parsley leaves

¾ cup fresh basil leaves, shredded

1. Pre-heat the pressure cooker using the BROWN setting.

2. Add the oil and sauté the onion until it starts to become tender – about 5 minutes. Add the rice, salt and pepper, pour in the water or chicken stock and lock the lid in place.

3. Pressure cook on HIGH for 20 minutes.

4. While the rice is cooking, prepare the vinaigrette. In a small bowl, combine the vinegar, honey, salt and freshly ground black pepper. Whisk in the olive oil and set aside.

5. Let the pressure drop NATURALLY and carefully remove the lid. Transfer the rice to a large salad bowl and fluff with a wooden spoon as you add the vinaigrette. Let the dressed rice cool for about 10 minutes.

6. Add all the remaining ingredients to the salad bowl and toss. Season to taste with salt and pepper and serve.

Vegetable Side Dishes

Cauliflower with Breadcrumbs and Lemon-Caper Vinaigrette

Creamy Maple Sweet Potatoes

Butternut Squash Purée with Orange and Honey

Beets and Potatoes with Bacon

Parsnip, Pear and Rosemary Mash

Potato Gratin

Steamed Artichokes

Roasted Red Pepper Aïoli

Tuna-Caper Aïoli

Chipotle Orange Aïoli

Cumin Carrots with Kale

Cauliflower with Breadcrumbs and Lemon-Caper Vinaigrette

This recipe is a win-win! It's super easy to make AND it's elegant and delicious. Maybe that makes it a win-win-win!

Serves
4

Cooking Time
12 to 15 Minutes

Release Method
Quick-release

1 head cauliflower

½ cup coarse fresh breadcrumbs

1 tablespoon butter or olive oil

1 tablespoon white wine vinegar

2 teaspoons capers, rinsed and rough chopped

1 teaspoon finely minced shallot

1 teaspoon lemon zest

2 tablespoons fresh lemon juice

¼ cup extra virgin olive oil

½ teaspoon salt

freshly ground black pepper

1 tablespoon chopped fresh parsley

1. Trim the cauliflower of any leaves and score the core of the cauliflower deeply - make two cuts into the core in a cross shape. Cut deeply, but not so deep that the cauliflower falls apart.

2. Place the cauliflower into the pressure cooker on a rack. Add 1 cup of water and lock the lid in place.

3. Pressure cook on HIGH for 12 to 15 minutes (depending on the size of the head of cauliflower and how tender you like your cauliflower).

4. While the cauliflower is cooking, toast the breadcrumbs in a skillet with either butter or olive oil until lightly brown. Make the vinaigrette by combining the remaining ingredients in a small bowl.

5. Release the pressure using the QUICK-RELEASE method and carefully remove the lid. Remove the cauliflower from the cooker and place it on a cutting board. Slice the cauliflower in large slices and fan the slices out on a serving dish. Scatter the breadcrumbs over the slices and drizzle the vinaigrette over the top.

Want to impress? Look for a purple cauliflower instead of the usual white version. It will cook a little faster than traditional cauliflower, so cook for the shorter amount of time. Regardless of color, choose a head of cauliflower with uniform colored florets, no blemishes, vibrant fresh leaves, and one that feels heavy for its size.

Creamy Maple Sweet Potatoes

Here's a quick and easy way to make a side dish for that all important family gathering we call Thanksgiving! Use your pressure cooker to make the sweet potatoes and leave your stovetop and oven free for all the other dishes that make up the year's biggest meal.

Serves
6

Cooking Time
4 Minutes

Release Method
Quick-release

3 pounds sweet potatoes, peeled and cut into 1-inch chunks

3 tablespoons butter

½ teaspoon ground cinnamon

¼ cup maple syrup

¼ cup heavy cream

salt and freshly ground black pepper

1. Place the potatoes into the pressure cooker and add enough water to just cover the vegetables. Lock the lid in place.

2. Pressure cook on HIGH for 4 minutes.

3. Release the pressure using the QUICK-RELEASE method and carefully remove the lid. Drain the potatoes and return them to the warm pressure cooker. Add the butter, cinnamon, maple syrup and heavy cream and mash the potatoes using a potato masher, a food mill or just smash them with a good wooden spoon. Season to taste with salt and freshly ground black pepper.

Top the finished potatoes with candied pecans to make this dish truly dinner-party worthy.

Butternut Squash Purée
with Orange and Honey

This is a bright and fresh side dish that is quick and super easy to make, and it goes with so many things. The butternut squash can be a little stringy if you mash it by hand. If you really want the purée smooth, be sure to use a food mill or ricer.

Serves
4

Cooking Time
5 Minutes

Release Method
Quick-release

1 butternut squash, peeled and chopped (about 5 to 6 cups)

1 Russet potato, peeled and chopped into 1-inch chunks

1 tablespoon butter

2 tablespoons honey

1 tablespoon orange zest

1 tablespoon chopped fresh thyme leaves

salt and freshly ground black pepper

1. Place the butternut squash and potato in the pressure cooker. Add enough water to just cover the vegetables and lock the lid in place.

2. Pressure cook on HIGH for 5 minutes.

3. Release the pressure using the QUICK-RELEASE method and carefully remove the lid. Drain the vegetables and return them to the warm pressure cooker. Add the butter, honey, orange zest and thyme leaves, and mash using a potato masher, a food mill or just smash them with a good wooden spoon. Season to taste with salt and freshly ground black pepper.

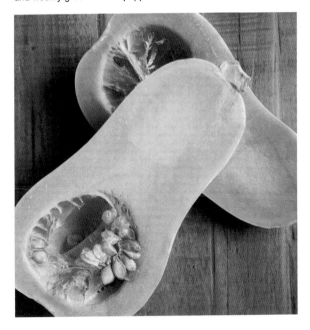

The hardest part of this recipe is peeling and chopping the butternut squash, so... why not buy it pre-peeled and chopped?

Beets and Potatoes with Bacon

The bright red color of this dish is striking and always gets noticed! The potatoes break down a little more than the beets do, which helps to bind this dish together. I love the smoky bacon flavor with the earthy beets, but if you want to make this vegetarian, just substitute 2 tablespoons of extra virgin olive oil.

Serves
4

Cooking Time
6 Minutes

Release Method
Quick-release

3 large beets, peeled and diced (½-inch dice) (about 5 cups)

2 large yellow potatoes, scrubbed and diced (1-inch dice) (about 5 cups)

4 strips of bacon, chopped

1 red onion, finely chopped

½ cup heavy cream

¼ cup chopped fresh parsley

salt and freshly ground black pepper

1. Place the beets and potatoes into the pressure cooker and add enough water to just cover the vegetables. Lock the lid in place.

2. Pressure cook on HIGH for 6 minutes.

3. While the potatoes and beets are cooking, pre-heat a large skillet over medium-high heat. Add the bacon and cook for about 5 minutes. Add the onion and sauté with the bacon until the onion starts to become tender – another 5 minutes.

4. Release the pressure using the QUICK-RELEASE method and carefully remove the lid.

5. Drain the beets and potatoes and transfer to a large serving bowl. Add the bacon and onions and toss well. Stir in the heavy cream and parsley, season to taste with salt and freshly ground black pepper and serve.

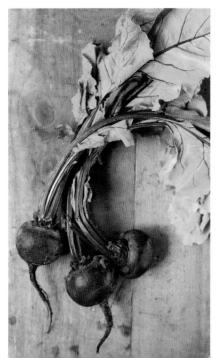

 Shortcut

You can make this a one-pot dish if you cook the bacon and onion in the pressure cooker on the BROWN setting and set it aside before step 1, but then what would you do during the quick six minutes it takes for the vegetables to cook? 😊

Parsnip, Pear and Rosemary Mash

If you don't like parsnips, this recipe might change your mind. The pear sweetens the parsnips so gently and the rosemary adds a nice herbaceous note. This is a great fresh alternative to mashed potatoes.

Serves
4

Cooking Time
4 Minutes

Release Method
Quick-release

1 pound parsnips, peeled and chopped

1 pear, peeled and chopped

1 sprig fresh rosemary

2 tablespoons butter

¼ cup heavy cream

salt and freshly ground black pepper

1 teaspoon finely chopped fresh rosemary

1. Add the parsnips, pear and rosemary sprig to the pressure cooker and add enough water to just cover the parsnips and pears and lock the lid in place.

2. Pressure cook on HIGH for 4 minutes.

3. Release the pressure using the QUICK-RELEASE method and carefully remove the lid. Drain the vegetables and return them to the warm pressure cooker, removing the rosemary sprig. Add the butter and cream, and mash the parsnips using a potato masher, a food mill or just smash them with a good wooden spoon. Season to taste with salt and freshly ground black pepper and serve with a little fresh rosemary.

The starches in parsnips convert to sugar in the cold. So, store your parsnips (dried of any moisture) in a plastic bag in the refrigerator crisper drawer. They should keep there for up to a month.

Potato Gratin

Being able to make potato gratin in the pressure cooker is a huge time saver. The liquid quantity in this recipe is at a minimum, so make sure as little liquid evaporates from the cooker as possible before pressure is reached. Stick around the kitchen while the pressure cooker is coming to pressure and push down firmly on the lid if any steam escapes from around the lid in the process. That will quickly form the seal needed to build pressure retaining the liquid inside.

Serves
6 to 8

Cooking Time
6 Minutes

Release Method
Quick-release

2 tablespoons butter

1 onion, finely chopped

2 cloves garlic, minced

1 tablespoon fresh thyme leaves

1 cup chicken or vegetable stock

1 cup heavy cream

2 teaspoons salt

lots of freshly ground black pepper

2 to 3 large Russet potatoes, peeled and thinly sliced (about 1 to 1½ pounds)

1 tablespoon butter

1 cup panko breadcrumbs

½ cup grated Parmesan cheese

fresh thyme for garnish

1. Pre-heat the pressure cooker using the BROWN setting.

2. Add the butter to the cooker and sauté the onion until it starts to become tender – about 5 minutes. Add the garlic and thyme and cook for another minute. Turn the cooker off, stir in the stock and heavy cream and season with salt and freshly ground black pepper. Then, add the potatoes, separating the slices so they don't stick together and each slice gets evenly coated in the liquid. The top layer of potatoes should be just partially covered in liquid. Lock the lid in place.

3. Pressure cook on HIGH for 6 minutes.

4. While the potatoes are cooking, heat a skillet over medium-high heat. Add the butter and toast the breadcrumbs in the skillet, tossing regularly. Set aside.

5. Release the pressure using the QUICK-RELEASE method and carefully remove the lid. Sprinkle the Parmesan cheese over the top of the potatoes and let the gratin cool with the lid off. The cheese will melt and the potatoes will absorb more liquid. Serve the gratin out of the pressure cooker on to plates and top with the reserved toasted breadcrumbs and fresh thyme.

Turn this dish from Pommes Dauphinoise (the fancy French way of saying potato gratin) into Pommes Boulangères by using more stock instead of the heavy cream.

Steamed Artichokes
with Dipping Sauces

You can't find fresh artichokes all year long (early spring is their prime season with a smaller harvest in the fall), but when you can they make a fun, interactive appetizer or snack along with a dip or two.

Serves
4

Cooking Time
12 Minutes

Release Method
Quick-release

4 medium artichokes

1 lemon

4 or 5 sprigs fresh thyme

Aïoli dipping sauce
(recipes on page 192)

1. Prepare the artichokes by cutting off the top inch of the prickly leaves. Cut off the stem to create a flat base and pull off any blemished outer leaves.

2. Place a rack in the pressure cooker and rest the artichokes on top of the rack. Squeeze the lemon juice all over the artichokes and drop the squeezed halves into the cooker around the artichokes along with the fresh thyme sprigs. Add 2 cups of water to the cooker and lock the lid in place.

3. Pressure cook on HIGH for 12 minutes.

4. Release the pressure using the QUICK-RELEASE method and carefully remove the lid. Before you transfer the artichokes to a serving dish, invert them over the pressure cooker to allow any hot water to escape from between the leaves. Serve with one or more of the dipping sauces.

When eating artichokes this way, you only eat the flesh at the bottom of the petal. Pull the petal off the artichoke, hold it by the tip and dip into the dipping sauce of your choice. Then pull the petal through your teeth, scraping off the soft, tender part and discarding the remainder. When you get to the center of the artichoke, scrape away the fuzzy inedible choke with a spoon and eat the heart which remains below.

Roasted Red Pepper Aïoli

Tuna Caper Aïoli

Chipotle Orange Aïoli

⅓ cup mayonnaise

1 clove garlic, minced and mashed into a paste

¼ cup chopped roasted red pepper (jarred is fine)

1 tablespoon chopped fresh parsley

2 tablespoons finely chopped toasted almonds

1 teaspoon red wine vinegar

⅛ teaspoon smoked paprika

¼ teaspoon salt

1. Mix all ingredients together in a bowl.

½ cup mayonnaise

1 clove garlic, minced and mashed into a paste

1 tablespoon lemon zest (about 1 lemon)

2 tablespoons capers, rinsed and chopped

1 can flaked tuna

2 tablespoons chopped fresh parsley

¼ teaspoon salt

freshly ground black pepper

1. Mix all ingredients together in a bowl.

⅓ cup mayonnaise

1 clove garlic, minced and mashed into a paste

1½ teaspoons orange zest

1 teaspoon chopped chipotle pepper in adobo

1 tablespoon finely chopped fresh cilantro

¼ teaspoons salt

1 teaspoon orange juice

1. Mix all ingredients together in a bowl.

Let's Veg

It's common knowledge that the less you cook vegetables, the more nutrients you retain in those vegetables. So, keeping the cooking time down by pressure-cooking is a good thing for veggies nutritionally, and it also helps them retain great flavor and color too.

Dense vegetables are best. You can cook any vegetable in the pressure cooker either by boiling or steaming it. The cooking time might be as little as one minute, but it can be done. You'll get more bang for your time-saving buck, however, if you choose to pressure-cook vegetables that tend to be more dense. Root vegetables and winter squash really show off a reduced cooking time in a pressure cooker.

Steaming vs. Boiling. Both methods work for vegetables in a pressure cooker, but steaming is a healthier technique. In order to steam vegetables, you will need a rack or steamer insert for the cooker.

Steaming racks and inserts. It is possible to find a steamer rack and basket to fit almost any size of pressure cooker, but you can also make your own version that will work sufficiently. Metal ring molds, cookie cutters or crumpled up and then rolled aluminum foil can serve as a rack to elevate foods. You can also use aluminum foil to make a steamer insert by shaping it into a basket and poking holes in the bottom. Silicone colanders (especially the collapsible kind) often fit into a pressure cooker and can be used to steam vegetables too.

Release it quickly! Vegetables generally have a short cooking time and can over-cook easily. For this reason, the quick-release method is used for vegetables. That puts a stop to the cooking time and you can test and retrieve your vegetables at their perfect stage of doneness. It also means that it's easy to add a minute or two of cooking time, should they be a little under-done.

Uniformity! I had a chef in culinary school who used to yell "Uniformité!" in his French accent around the kitchen. To this day, I think of Chef Michel every time I cut up vegetables. In order to cook vegetables properly, they all need to be the same or similar size whether you're using traditional cooking methods or pressure-cooking.

Cumin Carrots with Kale

Sometimes the little things make all the difference. In this recipe, cutting the carrots on the bias makes them so much more attractive than cutting them into straight slices. An easy way to cut all the carrots uniformly is to hold the carrot with each end pointing at eleven and five o'clock and keep the knife moving between six and twelve o'clock.

Serves
6 to 8

Cooking Time
2 to 3 Minutes

Release Method
Quick-release

1 tablespoon olive oil

1 teaspoon cumin seeds

2 pounds carrots, sliced on the bias (½-inch thick)

3 cups chopped kale

1 teaspoon salt

freshly ground black pepper

1 cup water

half a lemon

coarse sea salt

1. Pre-heat the pressure cooker using the BROWN setting.

2. Add the olive oil and toast the cumin seeds until they are fragrant – about 2 minutes. Add the carrots and stir well, cooking for another 2 minutes. Stir in the kale and coat with oil. Season to taste with salt and freshly ground black pepper and pour in the water. Lock the lid in place.

3. Pressure cook on HIGH for 2 to 3 minutes, depending on how cooked you like your carrots.

4. Release the pressure using the QUICK-RELEASE method and carefully remove the lid. Remove the carrots and kale with a slotted spoon (or pour into a strainer) and transfer to a serving bowl or plate. Dress the carrots with a squeeze of lemon juice and some coarse sea salt.

Dress It Up

If you can get your hands on multi-colored carrots, mix them all together in this recipe for a colorful side dish.

Breakfast

Ham and Cheddar Grits

Quinoa Porridge with Banana, Apricots and Almonds

Steel-Cut Oats with Apples and Raisins

Blueberry Polenta with Bananas and Maple Syrup

Breakfast Risotto with Bacon, Eggs and Tomatoes

Tropical Morning Rice Pudding

Compotes for pancakes and more...Blackberry Pear Compote

Strawberry Pomegranate Compote

Maple Apple Blueberry Compote

Ham and Cheddar Grits

I'm far from being a Southerner, but I have to admit that grits in the morning are satisfying and delicious, no matter how you dress them up. The nice thing about cooking them in a pressure cooker is that you don't have to stand over them stirring while they cook.

Serves
4

Cooking Time
10 Minutes

Release Method
Natural

2 tablespoons butter

4½ cups water

1 cup coarse corn grits (not the instant variety)

1 teaspoon salt

7-ounce ham steak, small dice

1½ cups grated Cheddar cheese

½ cup milk (optional)

freshly ground black pepper or crushed red pepper flakes

chopped fresh chives

1. Bring the butter and water to a boil in the pressure cooker using the BROWN setting.

2. Whisk in the grits and salt and continue to whisk for a full minute so that the grits have a moment to become suspended in the water rather than sinking to the bottom of the cooker. Lock the lid in place.

3. Pressure cook on HIGH for 10 minutes.

4. Let the pressure drop NATURALLY and carefully remove the lid. Stir in the ham and cheese and season to taste with salt and lots of freshly ground black pepper. Stir in the milk to thin the grits a little and cool them to an edible temperature. Sprinkle chives on top and serve.

While the grits are cooking, sauté some shrimp (peeled, deveined and tails removed) in olive oil with garlic and crushed red pepper flakes. At the very end of cooking, add a pinch of smoked paprika and a squeeze of lemon. Top the finished grits with the shrimp and call it a meal!

Quinoa Porridge
with Banana, Apricots and Almonds

A bowl of quinoa porridge is a great way to start the day. It's high in protein and will keep you more full and satiated for longer. You can add any fruit, fresh or dried to mix it up from day to day.

Serves
2 to 3

Cooking Time
7 Minutes

Release Method
Quick-release

1 tablespoon butter

¾ cup quinoa, rinsed

1¼ cups water or almond milk

½ banana, sliced

⅓ cup chopped dried apricots

pinch of ground nutmeg

pinch of salt

chopped toasted almonds

1. Combine all the ingredients, except for the almonds, in the pressure cooker and lock the lid in place.

2. Pressure cook on HIGH for 7 minutes.

3. Release the pressure using the QUICK-RELEASE method and carefully remove the lid.

4. Stir and let the porridge sit for a few minutes to continue to absorb moisture and to cool to an edible temperature. Stir a little more almond milk in to thin the porridge if necessary, and top with the toasted almonds.

Substitution

If you choose to use almond milk in this recipe, pay attention to whether you use sweetened or unsweetened almond milk. You may want the porridge to have a sweet flavor, but the bananas and apricots really make it quite sweet on their own.

Steel-Cut Oats with Apples and Raisins

SUPER EASY

VEGETARIAN

I like my steel-cut oats with a little of the chewiness left in. I think it makes them more interesting, but if you don't share my opinion, add a couple of minutes to this cooking time.

Serves
2

Cooking Time
5 Minutes

Release Method
Natural

1 tablespoon butter

¾ cup steel cut oats

2 cups water

1 Granny Smith apple, chopped (peeled or unpeeled)

⅓ cup raisins

¼ teaspoon ground cinnamon

good pinch of salt

1. Combine all the ingredients in the pressure cooker and lock the lid in place.

2. Pressure cook on HIGH for 5 minutes.

3. Let the pressure drop NATURALLY and carefully remove the lid.

4. Stir and let the oats sit for a few minutes to continue to absorb moisture and to cool to an edible temperature. Thin with water or milk if necessary, and top with a little maple syrup, a dollop of Greek yogurt or some chopped toasted nuts.

Did You Know...?

Don't omit the butter in this recipe. It's there for more than just flavor. Whenever you're cooking something that has a tendency to foam, you always want to have butter or oil to keep the foaming under control. Also, make sure your cooker is less than half full when making this recipe.

Blueberry Polenta
with Bananas and Maple Syrup

You may not think about polenta for breakfast, but it's almost the same as having a bowl of grits (see 'Did You Know?" below). This version is beautiful with streaks of blue breaking up the yellow polenta.

Serves
4

Cooking Time
5 Minutes

Release Method
Quick-release

2 tablespoons butter

4 cups water

1 cup polenta

pinch salt

2 tablespoons brown sugar

1½ cups blueberries

2 bananas, sliced

¼ cup half-and-half (or whole milk or heavy cream)

maple syrup

1. Bring the butter and water to a boil in the pressure cooker using the BROWN setting.

2. Whisk in the polenta, salt and brown sugar, and continue to whisk for a full minute so that the polenta has a moment to become suspended in the water rather than sinking to the bottom of the cooker. Lock the lid in place.

3. Pressure cook on HIGH For 5 minutes.

4. Release the pressure using the QUICK-RELEASE method and carefully remove the lid. Stir in the blueberries, bananas and half-and-half, heat through and let a few of them bleed into the polenta making a beautiful blue swirl in the yellow polenta. Serve with maple syrup on top.

Did You Know...?

The difference between polenta and grits is very small. Grits are made from "dent" corn and cook up creamy, whereas polenta is made from "flint" corn and retains some of its granular texture after being cooked.

Breakfast Risotto with Bacon, Eggs and Tomatoes

This is a dish you might serve for a weekend brunch, somewhere between breakfast and lunch. It's definitely filling enough to substitute for both those meals.

Serves
2 to 3

Cooking Time
7 Minutes

Release Method
Quick-release

6 slices of thick-sliced bacon, chopped

½ cup finely chopped onion

¾ cup Arborio or Carnaroli rice

½ cup chicken stock

1½ cups water

salt and freshly ground black pepper

2 eggs, lightly beaten

1 cup halved cherry tomatoes

¼ cup grated Cheddar cheese,
plus more for garnish

1. Pre-heat the pressure cooker using the BROWN setting.

2. Add the bacon and cook until almost crispy. Remove the bacon from the cooker with a slotted spoon and set aside. Drain all but 1 tablespoon of bacon fat from the cooker. Add the onion and cook the onion until it starts to become tender - about 5 minutes. Add the rice and stir to coat with the bacon fat. Pour in the chicken stock and water, season with salt and freshly ground black pepper and lock the lid in place.

3. Pressure cook on HIGH for 7 minutes.

4. Release the pressure using the QUICK-RELEASE method and carefully remove the lid. Immediately stir in the eggs. The residual heat from the risotto will be enough to cook them. Stir in the cherry tomatoes, reserved bacon and Cheddar cheese. Season to taste again with salt and freshly ground black pepper and serve with a little more grated Cheddar if desired.

 Did You Know...?

You can use either Arborio or Carnaroli rice for risotto. The lesser-known Carnaroli rice is a medium-grained rice with higher starch content, firmer texture and a longer grain than Arborio rice, which is a short-grain rice.

Tropical Morning Rice Pudding

Sometimes when it is cold outside, I like to throw some tropical flavors into whatever I'm eating to escape the weather. With the pineapple, mango, banana and coconut in this rice pudding, you can shut the door on winter... at least during breakfast.

Serves
2

Cooking Time
15 Minutes

Release Method
Quick-release

1 (14-ounce) can coconut milk

½ cup half and half

½ cup water

2 tablespoons granulated sugar

¾ cup long-grain rice

¼ cup dried pineapple

¼ cup chopped dried mango

toasted shredded coconut

½ banana, sliced

1. Place all ingredients except for the shredded coconut and banana into the pressure cooker. Stir well and lock the lid in place.

2. Pressure cook on HIGH for 15 minutes.

3. Release the pressure using the QUICK-RELEASE method and carefully remove the lid. Stir again, let the rice pudding cool to an edible temperature, and serve with the toasted coconut and banana on top.

Did You Know...?

You can toast shredded coconut in the oven *or* on the stovetop. On the stovetop, place the coconut into a large skillet and cook over medium heat, tossing as it browns. In the oven, place a layer of the shredded coconut on a cookie sheet and toast for about 5 to 10 minutes at 325° F.

Blackberry Pear Compote

This compote has a sweet-tart note to it. It is sweetened with apple juice and has no added sugar. If you want it a little sweeter, just add a little sugar or agave syrup at the end.

Makes
5 cups

Cooking Time
6 Minutes

Release Method
Natural

1 cup apple juice

4 pears, peeled and diced

20 ounces frozen blackberries (about 5 cups)

1 cinnamon stick

4 strips orange peel, 3-inches long

3 tablespoons cornstarch

2 tablespoons cold water

1. Combine all the ingredients except for the cornstarch and water in the pressure cooker and lock the lid in place.

2. Pressure cook on HIGH for 6 minutes, depending on the ripeness of the pears.

3. Let the pressure drop NATURALLY and carefully remove the lid. Combine the cornstarch and water in a small bowl and then stir it into the compote. Use the BROWN setting to bring the compote back to a simmer to thicken and then immediately turn off the heat. Let the compote cool to an edible temperature and remember to remove the cinnamon stick and orange peel before serving over pancakes, waffles, French toast, yogurt and granola or even over ice cream.

Pears bought at the grocery store are rarely perfectly ripe. To ripen them faster at home, store them in a paper bag. The pears give off ethylene gas, which ripens fruit. By trapping the gas, the pears will ripen faster. If you put another ethylene-producing fruit in the bag with the pears (like an apple, banana or an avocado), the pears will ripen even faster!

Strawberry Pomegranate Compote

The nice thing about this compote is that it calls for frozen strawberries. That makes it super easy to make – you don't have to hull and chop the berries and you don't have to wait for perfect strawberry season to make the tastiest compote. Of course, you CAN use fresh strawberries if it is perfect strawberry season!

Makes
3½ cups

Cooking Time
8 Minutes

Release Method
Natural

1 cup pomegranate juice

2 pounds frozen strawberries (about 6 cups)

½ cup sugar

zest of 2 lemons

3 tablespoons cornstarch

juice of 1 lemon

Seeds of 1 pomegranate (about ½ - ¾ cup)

1. Combine the pomegranate juice, strawberries, sugar and lemon zest in the pressure cooker and lock the lid in place.

2. Pressure cook on HIGH for 8 minutes.

3. While the compote is cooking, pick the seeds out of the pomegranate. For an easy tip on how to do this, see page 166.

4. Let the pressure drop NATURALLY and carefully remove the lid. Combine the cornstarch and lemon juice in a small bowl and then stir this into the compote. Use the BROWN setting to bring the compote back to a simmer to thicken and then immediately turn off the heat. Stir in the fresh pomegranate seeds and let the compote cool to an edible temperature before serving over pancakes, waffles, French toast, yogurt and granola or even over ice cream.

Maple Apple Blueberry Compote

There are so many varieties of apples to choose from, but some that work well in this recipe are Jonagold, Fuji, Pippin, and Pink Lady.

Makes
about 6 cups

Cooking Time
8 Minutes

Release Method
Natural

1 cup apple juice

4 apples, peeled and chopped

20 ounces frozen blueberries (about 4½ cups)

¼ cup maple syrup

½ teaspoon ground cinnamon

⅓ cup sugar

juice of 1 lemon

3 tablespoons cornstarch

2 tablespoons water

1. Combine all the ingredients except for the cornstarch and water in the pressure cooker and lock the lid in place.

2. Pressure cook on HIGH for 8 minutes.

3. Let the pressure drop NATURALLY and carefully remove the lid. Combine the cornstarch and water in a small bowl and then stir this into the compote. Use the BROWN setting to bring the compote back to a simmer to thicken and then immediately turn off the heat. Let the compote cool to an edible temperature before serving over pancakes, waffles, French toast, yogurt and granola or even over ice cream.

Dessert

Chocolate Raspberry Almond Torte

Crème Caramel with Orange and Hazelnuts

Blackberry Croissant Bread Pudding

Brown Sugar Bourbon Bread Pudding

Banana Cake with Chocolate Chunks

Carrot Cake with Cream Cheese Icing

White Chocolate Raspberry Rice Pudding

Carrot Cake Rice Pudding

Pudding Chômeur

Lemon Blueberry Cheesecake

Peanut Butter Cheesecake

Cherry Cheesecake with Dark Chocolate Ganache

Chocolate Raspberry Almond Torte

This almost flourless torte is not dense, but light in texture and not overly sweet. With a dollop of whipped cream it makes a nice, civilized, but decadent dessert.

Serves
6 to 8

Cooking Time
30 Minutes

Release Method
Combo

6 ounces semi-sweet chocolate, chopped

½ cup butter

3 eggs

½ teaspoon pure vanilla extract

⅓ cup sugar

¼ cup all-purpose flour

1 cup frozen raspberries, defrosted and drained

toasted sliced almonds, fresh raspberries, powdered sugar and heavy cream, for serving

1. Butter a 7-inch cake pan.

2. Melt the chocolate and butter together, either in the microwave or in a double boiler.

3. In a separate bowl, beat the eggs vigorously until they are thick and fall from the beater in one solid line like a ribbon. Whisk the vanilla extract and sugar into the eggs. Drizzle in the chocolate and butter, mixing well. Stir in the flour, combining until there are no lumps. Finally, fold in the raspberries. Pour the batter into the buttered cake pan and then wrap the pan completely in buttered aluminum foil.

4. Place a rack in the bottom of the pressure cooker and add 2 cups of water. Lower the cake pan into the cooker using a sling made of aluminum foil (fold a piece of aluminum foil into a strip about 2-inches wide by 24-inches long). Fold the ends of the aluminum foil into the cooker and lock the lid in place.

5. Pressure cook on HIGH for 30 minutes.

6. Let the pressure drop NATURALLY for 10 minutes. Then, release any residual pressure using the QUICK-RELEASE method and carefully remove the lid. Remove the cake pan from the cooker and let it cool. Invert the cake onto a serving plate. Sprinkle the toasted almonds, fresh raspberries and powdered sugar on top and serve with a dollop of whipped cream.

Did You Know...?

Mix a little crème fraîche into your heavy cream for a whipped topping that won't deflate over time. Crème fraîche is a soured cream that you can find in specialty dairy sections, and its high butterfat content (higher than heavy cream) helps to hold the whipped air pockets in whipped cream. It also has a nice tang to it that really compliments the chocolate raspberry almond torte.

Crème Caramel
with Orange and Hazelnuts

Crème Caramel works so well in a pressure cooker. The texture is perfect and you can flavor it with any ingredient you like at the end by sprinkling some chocolate, some shredded coconut, lemon zest or even dried lavender on top. Conversely, for a plain Crème Caramel, just omit the orange and hazelnut included here.

Serves
8

Cooking Time
12 Minutes

Release Method
Natural

¾ cup sugar

¼ cup water

1 cup whole milk

2 (3-inch) strips of orange peel

3 eggs

2 egg yolks

¼ cup sugar

1 teaspoon pure vanilla extract

1 cup heavy cream

¼ cup chopped toasted hazelnuts

1 tablespoon finely chopped orange zest

1. Combine the sugar and water in a saucepan over medium heat, stirring to dissolve the sugar. Increase the heat and bring the mixture to a boil. Stop stirring and instead swirl the pan every once in a while, as the sugar starts to brown and turn a deep amber color. As soon as it is a nice caramel color, remove it from the heat immediately and carefully pour the caramel into a 7-inch cake pan.

2. In a second saucepan, bring the milk and the orange peel to a simmer, stirring to prevent it from burning on the bottom, and then remove it from the heat and set it aside. In a separate bowl, beat the eggs, egg yolks, sugar and vanilla extract until the mixture is smooth and falls from the whisk in a line like a ribbon. Remove the orange peel from the milk and stir in the heavy cream. Whisk the milk and cream mixture into the egg mixture. Pour the mixture into the cake pan lined with the caramel and wrap tightly in aluminum foil.

3. Place a rack in the bottom of the pressure cooker and add 2 cups of water. Lower the cake pan into the cooker using a sling made of aluminum foil (fold a piece of aluminum foil into a strip about 2-inches wide by 24-inches long). Fold the ends of the aluminum foil into the cooker and lock the lid in place.

4. Pressure cook on HIGH for 12 minutes.

5. Let the pressure drop NATURALLY and carefully remove the lid. Remove the pan from the cooker and unwrap it. It should still jiggle a little in the very center. Cool to room temperature or wrap it with plastic wrap and refrigerate to serve later. When you are ready to serve, carefully run a butter knife around the side of the cake pan and invert the custard onto a plate. Sprinkle the top with the hazelnuts and orange zest before serving.

Blackberry Croissant Bread Pudding

I'm not sure if this should be breakfast or dessert! Either way, it's bound to please. If you don't have blackberries, this is great with raspberries or blueberries instead. No matter what berry you choose, it's a delicious way to use up old croissants.

Serves
8

Cooking Time
25 Minutes

Release Method
Natural

1 cup milk

1 cup heavy cream (plus more for serving if desired)

¾ cup granulated or brown sugar

1 vanilla bean, split open OR
1 teaspoon pure vanilla extract

1 teaspoon ground cinnamon

¼ cup blackberry preserves

4 eggs

8 croissants (day old are perfect; otherwise, slice the croissants in half horizontally and leave out on the countertop to dry)

1 cup fresh blackberries

½ cup sliced almonds, toasted

powdered sugar

1. Grease a 2-quart ceramic soufflé dish or metal baking pan with butter.

2. Combine the milk, heavy cream, sugar, vanilla bean, cinnamon and blackberry preserves in a saucepan and bring to a simmer, stirring to dissolve the sugar. Lightly beat the eggs in a bowl. Temper the eggs into the milk mixture by adding a little milk to the eggs, beating, and then adding the eggs back into the milk mixture. Remove custard from the heat.

3. Cut the croissants into quarters or large chunks and transfer them to a big bowl. Add the custard to the bowl and soak the croissants for about 5 minutes. Build the bread pudding by layering some of the soaked croissants with the some of the fresh blackberries and repeating until the casserole dish is full. Wrap the soufflé dish tightly with buttered aluminum foil.

4. Place a rack in the bottom of the pressure cooker and add 2 cups of water. Lower the cake pan into the cooker using a sling made of aluminum foil (fold a piece of aluminum foil into a strip about 2-inches wide by 24-inches long). Fold the ends of the aluminum foil into the cooker and lock the lid in place.

5. Pressure cook on HIGH for 25 minutes.

6. Let the pressure drop NATURALLY and carefully remove the lid. Remove the pudding from the cooker and let it cool. This can be served warm or cold with the almonds and powdered sugar scattered on top.

When blackberries are in season (late summer through early fall) they can be sweet and delicious. If they are not in season, however, you can get quite a tart surprise when you bite down. If you can't find delicious blackberries, substitute any other berry in this recipe.

Brown Sugar Bourbon Bread Pudding

To me, bread puddings are the comfort food of the dessert world. I prefer them served warm, with cool whipped cream melting on top… but I have to admit I've also been known to enjoy day old bread pudding the morning after!

Serves
8

Cooking Time
25 Minutes

Release Method
Natural

½ cup raisins

½ cup bourbon

1 cup milk

1 cup heavy cream (plus more for serving if desired)

3 eggs

¾ cup brown sugar

1 vanilla bean, split open OR 1 teaspoon pure vanilla extract

1 teaspoon ground cinnamon

pinch ground nutmeg

7 cups cubed stale brioche, Challah, or any dense white bread

1 cup heavy cream

1. Combine the raisins and bourbon in a small saucepan and bring to a boil. Simmer for a couple of minutes and then remove from the heat and set aside.

2. Grease a 7-inch metal cake pan or a 2-quart ceramic soufflé dish with butter.

3. Combine the milk, heavy cream, eggs, brown sugar, vanilla bean, cinnamon and nutmeg in a bowl, stirring to dissolve the sugar. Pour this custard over the brioche cubes and let the bread soak up the custard for 10 minutes. Remove the raisins from the bourbon with a slotted spoon and toss them gently into the soaked brioche. Transfer the brioche to the cake pan and wrap the pan tightly with buttered aluminum foil.

4. Place a rack in the bottom of the pressure cooker and add 2 cups of water. Lower the cake pan into the cooker using a sling made of aluminum foil (fold a piece of aluminum foil into a strip about 2-inches wide by 24-inches long). Fold the ends of the aluminum foil into the cooker and lock the lid in place.

5. Pressure cook on HIGH for 25 minutes.

6. Let the pressure drop NATURALLY and carefully remove the lid. Remove the pudding from the cooker and let it cool. Combine the remaining bourbon with the heavy cream and whip lightly. Serve the bread pudding with a little of the bourbon cream.

 Substitution

No bourbon? No problem! You can soak the raisins in rum, or if you want to avoid the alcohol altogether, try soaking them in a little non-alcoholic vanilla extract or sparkling cranberry juice.

Banana Cake
with Chocolate Chunks

Making cakes in the pressure cooker doesn't always speed up the time it takes to bake them, but it certainly keeps the cakes moist and delicious. The layers of chocolate in the center and on the top of this cake really make this cake look decadent, and in this case, looks are NOT deceiving!

Serves
6 to 8

Cooking Time
50 Minutes

Release Method
Natural

½ cup butter, melted
(1 stick or 4 ounces)

1 cup granulated sugar

1 egg

1 teaspoon pure vanilla extract

4 ripe bananas, mashed (about 1 cup)

½ cup sour cream

1 teaspoon baking soda

1½ cups all-purpose flour

1 teaspoon baking powder

¼ teaspoon salt

1 cup semi-sweet or bitter-sweet chocolate chunks

¼ cup brown sugar

¼ teaspoon ground cinnamon

1. Butter a 7-inch cake pan.

2. Mix the melted butter, sugar, egg, vanilla extract and bananas together in a large bowl. In a second bowl, combine the sour cream and the baking soda. In a third bowl, combine the flour, baking powder and salt. Finally, in a fourth bowl, combine the chocolate chunks, brown sugar and cinnamon. Add the flour mixture to the butter mixture, alternating with the sour cream mixture. Pour half of the batter into the buttered cake pan. Scatter half of the chocolate chip mixture on top. Cover with the remaining batter and then sprinkle the remaining chocolate chip mixture on top. Wrap the pan completely in a piece of well-greased aluminum foil.

3. Place a rack in the bottom of the pressure cooker and add 2 cups of water. Lower the cake pan into the cooker using a sling made of aluminum foil (fold a piece of aluminum foil into a strip about 2-inches wide by 24-inches long). Fold the ends of the aluminum foil into the cooker and lock the lid in place.

4. Pressure cook on HIGH for 50 minutes.

5. Let the pressure drop NATURALLY and carefully remove the lid. Remove the cake pan from the cooker and let it cool. Transfer the cake to a serving plate and serve with a dollop of whipped cream if desired.

If you're craving banana cake RIGHT NOW, and don't have any bananas on hand, all is not lost! You can speed-ripen your bananas by popping them into a 300°F oven for 30 to 40 minutes (still in their peels). Line the baking sheet with some parchment first – the bananas have a tendency to leak a little as they "ripen".

Carrot Cake
with Cream Cheese Icing

Carrot cake is one of my favorite non-chocolate cakes (because chocolate almost always takes the cake in my world!). You can ice the entire cake with the cream cheese icing if you like, but I prefer to dollop some icing on the plate next to a slice of carrot cake. That way, I can scoop up a little icing with every bite!

Serves
6 to 8

Cooking Time
45 Minutes

Release Method
Natural

1¼ cups all-purpose flour

1 teaspoon baking powder

½ teaspoon baking soda

1 teaspoon ground cinnamon

¼ teaspoon ground nutmeg

¼ teaspoon salt

3 to 4 medium carrots
(about ½ pound), grated

¼ cup raisins (optional)

¾ cup granulated sugar

¼ cup brown sugar

2 eggs

¾ cup canola or vegetable oil

For the icing:

8 ounces cream cheese, softened at room temperature

8 tablespoons butter (4 ounces or 1 stick), softened at room temperature

1 cup powdered sugar

1 teaspoon pure vanilla extract

1. Butter a 7-inch cake pan.

2. Combine the dry ingredients in a bowl. Add the grated carrots and raisins (if using) and toss well. In a separate bowl, beat the sugars and eggs together until light and frothy. Drizzle in the oil, beating constantly. Fold the egg mixture into the dry ingredients until everything is just combined and you no longer see any traces of flour. Pour the batter into the cake pan and wrap the pan completely in greased aluminum foil.

3. Place a rack in the bottom of the pressure cooker and add 2 cups of water. Lower the cake pan into the cooker using a sling made of aluminum foil (fold a piece of aluminum foil into a strip about 2-inches wide by 24-inches long). Fold the ends of the aluminum foil into the cooker and lock the lid in place.

4. Pressure cook on HIGH for 45 minutes.

5. While the cake is cooking, beat the cream cheese, butter, powdered sugar and vanilla extract together using a hand mixer, stand mixer or food processor (or a lot of elbow grease!).

6. Let the pressure drop NATURALLY and carefully remove the lid. Remove the cake pan from the cooker and let it cool. Transfer the cake to a serving plate and serve with a dollop of the cream cheese frosting.

 Shortcut

The fastest way to make this cake is to use a food processor. Use the grating blades to grate the carrots and then transfer them to the dry ingredient bowl. No need to clean the bowl, just go right ahead and use the regular blade in the food processor to whip up the wet ingredients, drizzling in the oil.

White Chocolate Raspberry
Rice Pudding

This is, without a doubt, one of the easiest desserts in the book to prepare. Just throw the ingredients into the pressure cooker and stir in the white chocolate and raspberries at the end. The fresh raspberries add a nice sweet-tart flavor to the rich creamy pudding.

Serves
8 to 10

Cooking Time
16 Minutes

Release Method
Quick-release

1½ cups short grain white rice

2 cups half and half

2 cups whole milk

½ cup sugar

½ teaspoon grated nutmeg

½ cup heavy cream

1 cup white chocolate, chopped
(plus more for garnish)

2 cups raspberries

1. Pre-heat the pressure cooker using the BROWN setting.

2. Place the rice, half and half, milk, sugar and nutmeg in the pressure cooker and lock the lid in place.

3. Pressure cook on HIGH for 16 minutes.

4. Release the pressure using the QUICK-RELEASE method and carefully remove the lid. Stir the heavy cream and white chocolate into the pudding just until it melts. Stir in the raspberries and let the berries warm and start to bleed a little, making splashes of red throughout the white pudding. Garnish the pudding with some shaved white chocolate and more raspberries if desired.

You *can* use frozen raspberries for this dessert, but be prepared for a change in color. Defrost the raspberries and strain away the liquid. When you stir them into the pudding, their color will bleed faster and you'll end up with a pink pudding – not a bad thing…

Carrot Cake Rice Pudding

I like the flavors in carrot cake so much I decided they'd be nice in a rice pudding as well! The carrots melt into the pudding and the cream cheese stirred in at the end gives the dish that familiar tang of the sweet cream cheese frosting we all love.

Serves
6 to 8

Cooking Time
16 Minutes

Release Method
Quick-release

1 tablespoon butter

2 cups grated carrot (about 4 carrots)

1½ cups short grain white rice

2 cups half and half

2 cups whole milk

½ cup sugar

1 teaspoon ground cinnamon

½ teaspoon grated nutmeg

½ teaspoon ground allspice

½ cup cream cheese, room temperature (4 ounces)

½ cup toasted chopped walnuts (optional)

1. Pre-heat the pressure cooker using the BROWN setting.

2. Add the butter and cook the carrots for a few minutes. Add the rice and stir well to coat all the kernels with the butter. Add the half and half, milk, sugar and the spices. Give it another good stir and lock the lid in place.

3. Pressure cook on HIGH for 16 minutes.

4. Release the pressure using the QUICK-RELEASE method and carefully remove the lid. Stir the cream cheese into the pudding just until it melts (I like to leave it a little chunky). Garnish the pudding with the toasted walnuts if desired.

Did You Know...?

Allspice is not a blend of spices, but an actual berry from a plant cultivated in warm climates. It's name comes from the fact that its flavor is reminiscent of cinnamon, cloves and nutmeg. So… if you can't find allspice for this recipe, you can substitute ¼ teaspoon ground cinnamon (in addition to what is already called for), and ¼ teaspoon ground cloves.

Pudding Chômeur

Pudding Chômeur is a traditional Quebeçois dessert that translates as "unemployment pudding" and was considered a poor man's dessert. Of course, with the prices of pure maple syrup that's not really true today, but using the real deal is the secret to the success of this super sweet dessert.

Serves
6 (makes 6 individual ramekins)

Cooking Time
25 Minutes

Release Method
Quick-release

1 cup pure maple syrup

1 cup heavy cream

½ cup brown sugar

½ cup butter

¼ cup granulated sugar

2 eggs

½ teaspoon pure vanilla extract

1½ cups all-purpose flour

½ teaspoon baking powder

¼ teaspoon salt

sour cream, crème fraîche or heavy cream, for serving (optional)

1. Combine the maple syrup, heavy cream and brown sugar in a small saucepan and bring to a boil. Remove from the heat.

2. Cream the butter and sugar together in a bowl with an electric mixer until light and fluffy. Add the eggs and vanilla extract and beat until just combined. Add the flour, baking powder and salt and mix until just combined (the batter will be thick like cookie dough).

3. Pour some of the maple syrup mixture into six 6-ounce ramekins, covering the bottom of each ramekin with about ½-inch of the liquid. Divide the batter into 6 chunks and place a chunk in each ramekin. Pour the remaining maple syrup mixture over and around the dough, filling the ramekins to the top. Wrap each ramekin completely with a piece of buttered aluminum foil.

4. Place a rack in the bottom of the pressure cooker and add 2 cups of water. Place the ramekins on the rack, stacking them on top of each other if necessary. Lock the lid in place.

5. Pressure cook on HIGH for 25 minutes.

6. Release the pressure using the QUICK-RELEASE method and carefully remove the lid. Remove the ramekins from the cooker and unwrap them. Let them cool to an edible temperature and then serve warm either alone or with a dollop of cream. (Remember this is a very sweet dessert and the sour cream or crème fraîche is surprisingly refreshing).

The darker the color of the maple syrup, the more maple flavor it has. Pick a nice amber colored maple syrup for this dessert so you get more bang for your buck.

Lemon Blueberry Cheesecake

This is the lightest cheesecake of the three recipes in the book. It has a bright lemony flavor that contrasts nicely with the sweet and creamy cheese. Remember, a cheesecake needs time to set up after cooking – at least 8 hours – so this is a dessert that you need to make for tomorrow, not today.

Serves
6 (makes one 7-inch cheesecake)

Cooking Time
22 Minutes + 8 Hours to cool

Release Method
Natural

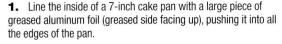

6 graham crackers, crushed

1 teaspoon finely grated lemon zest

2 tablespoons butter, melted

1 cup fresh or frozen blueberries, plus more for garnish

1 to 2 tablespoons sugar (depending on the sweetness of the blueberries)

1 teaspoon cornstarch

Juice of ½ a lemon

16 ounces (1 pound) cream cheese, room temperature

⅔ cup sugar

1 tablespoon lemon juice

2 teaspoons finely grated lemon zest

2 eggs

1. Line the inside of a 7-inch cake pan with a large piece of greased aluminum foil (greased side facing up), pushing it into all the edges of the pan.

2. Crush the graham crackers and the lemon zest together in a food processor until they form fine crumbs. Mix the crumbs with the butter and press the crumb mixture into the base of the cake pan. Refrigerate while you prepare the cheesecake batter.

3. Place the blueberries, sugar, cornstarch and juice of half a lemon in a small saucepan and bring to a boil. Stir, crushing the blueberries as you go, and simmer until the sauce has thickened slightly. Let the blueberries cool and then transfer them to a zipper sealable bag.

4. Using the paddle on your stand mixer with low speed, or the regular beaters on a hand mixer on low speed, or a food processor (scraping the sides of the processor bowl several times) blend the cream cheese until it is completely smooth with no lumps. When all the lumps in the cream cheese have disappeared, add the sugar, lemon juice and lemon zest. Blend to incorporate the ingredients and then add the eggs one at a time, mixing only to distribute the eggs evenly in the batter. Do not over-mix at this point.

5. Pour half the batter into the cake pan with the graham cracker crust. Cut a corner off the zipper sealable bag with the blueberry mixture and drizzle half the blueberry mixture over the cheesecake in a zigzag pattern. Run a knife through the sauce, perpendicular to the zigzags to create a swirl look. Repeat with the remaining cheesecake batter and blueberries, making a pretty swirl pattern on top. Cover the pan tightly with more greased aluminum foil.

6. Place a rack in the bottom of the pressure cooker and add 2 cups of water. Lower the cake pan into the cooker using a sling made of aluminum foil (fold a piece of aluminum foil into a strip about 2-inches wide by 24-inches long). Fold the ends of the aluminum foil into the cooker and lock the lid in place.

7. Pressure cook on HIGH for 22 minutes.

8. Let the pressure drop NATURALLY and let the cheesecake sit in the turned off pressure cooker for one hour. Carefully remove the lid and transfer the cheesecake from the cooker to the counter using the aluminum sling or rack. Let the cheesecake come to room temperature and then remove the foil from the top of the cake pan. Blot any liquid that might have condensed on the surface of the cake, wrap it in plastic wrap and refrigerate for at least 8 hours.

9. Bring the cake to room temperature before serving, and serve with more fresh blueberries and lemon zest if desired.

Peanut Butter Cheesecake

There are a few steps to making this cheesecake, but if you do all the suggested decorations at the end, you'll end up with a dessert that will look like it came from a high-end bakery. It's over-the-top delicious!

Serves
6 (makes one 7-inch cheesecake)

Cooking Time
22 Minutes + 8 Hours to cool

Release Method
Natural

10 peanut butter sandwich cookies, crushed

3 tablespoons butter, melted

16 ounces (1 pound) cream cheese, room temperature

⅔ cup sugar

2 eggs

⅓ cup creamy peanut butter

12 peanut butter cups, diced, divided

¾ cup hot fudge sauce

1. Line the inside of a 7-inch cake pan with a large piece of greased aluminum foil (greased side facing up), pushing it into all the edges of the pan.

2. Crush the cookies in a food processor until they form fine crumbs. Mix the crumbs with the melted butter and press the crumb mixture into the base of the cake pan. Refrigerate while you prepare the cheesecake batter.

3. Using the paddle on your stand mixer with low speed, or the regular beaters on a hand mixer on low speed, or a food processor (scraping the sides of the processor bowl several times) blend the cream cheese until it is completely smooth with no lumps. When all the lumps in the cream cheese have disappeared, add the sugar. Blend to incorporate the sugar and then add the eggs one at a time, mixing only enough to distribute the eggs in evenly in the batter.

4. Remove 1 cup of the cheesecake batter and place in a small bowl. Add the creamy peanut butter and stir until combined. Set this peanut butter batter aside.

5. Add one cup of the chopped peanut butter cups to the remaining cheesecake batter. Gently fold until evenly distributed. Pour cheesecake batter into prepared pan with cookie crust.

6. Dollop the peanut butter cheesecake mixture over the top of the batter in the pan. Gently spread the mixture evenly to smooth it over and to cover the top of the cake. Cover the pan tightly with more greased aluminum foil.

7. Place a rack in the bottom of the pressure cooker and add 2 cups of water. Lower the cake pan into the cooker using a sling made of aluminum foil (fold a piece of aluminum foil into a strip about 2-inches wide by 24-inches long). Fold the ends of the aluminum foil into the cooker and lock the lid in place.

8. Pressure cook on HIGH for 22 minutes.

9. Let the pressure drop NATURALLY and let the cheesecake sit in the turned off pressure cooker for one hour. Carefully remove the lid and transfer the cheesecake from the cooker to the counter using the aluminum sling or rack. Let the cheesecake come to room temperature and then remove the foil from the top of the cake pan. Blot any liquid that might have condensed on the surface of the cake, wrap it in plastic wrap and refrigerate for at least 8 hours.

10. Melt the hot fudge sauce in the microwave for about 30 seconds. Drizzle hot fudge across cheesecake and top with remaining chopped peanut butter cups. Bring the cheesecake to room temperature before serving. Dig in!

Use a warm butter knife to smooth out any wrinkles from the aluminum foil around the edges of the cheesecake. Just run the knife under hot water and then run it around the sides of the cake.

Cherry Cheesecake
with Dark Chocolate Ganache

This cake can be topped with frozen cherries OR pitted fresh cherries if they are in season. The fresh cherries make the top a little prettier, but no matter whether you use fresh or frozen, the result will be spectacular.

Serves
6 (makes one 7-inch cheesecake)

Cooking Time
22 Minutes + 8 Hours to cool

Release Method
Natural

10 chocolate sandwich cookies, crushed

2 tablespoons butter, melted

16 ounces (1 pound) cream cheese, room temperature

²/₃ cup sugar

2 eggs

1 cup frozen cherries, thawed and chopped

¾ cup dark chocolate chips

Dark Chocolate Ganache:

1 cup heavy cream,

1 cup dark chocolate chips

½ teaspoon pure vanilla extract

12 whole cherries, pitted, frozen or fresh

1. Line the inside of a 7-inch cake pan with a large piece of greased aluminum foil (greased side facing up), pushing it into all the edges of the pan.

2. Crush chocolate cookies in a food processor until they form a fine crumb. Mix the crumbs with the melted butter and press the crumb mixture into the base of the cake pan. Refrigerate while you prepare the cheesecake batter.

3. Using the paddle on your stand mixer with low speed, or the regular beaters on a hand mixer on low speed, or a food processor (scraping the sides of the processor bowl several times) blend the cream cheese until it is completely smooth with no lumps. When all the lumps in the cream cheese have disappeared, add the sugar. Blend to incorporate the sugar and then add the eggs one at a time, blending only to mix the eggs in evenly. Stir in the chopped cherries and their juice until combined and then stir in the dark chocolate chips. Pour the batter into the cake pan with the chocolate cookie crust. Cover the pan tightly with more greased aluminum foil.

4. Place a rack in the bottom of the pressure cooker and add 2 cups of water. Lower the cake pan into the cooker using a sling made of aluminum foil (fold a piece of aluminum foil into a strip about 2-inches wide by 24-inches long). Fold the ends of the aluminum foil into the cooker and lock the lid in place.

5. Pressure cook on HIGH for 22 minutes.

6. Let the pressure drop NATURALLY and let the cheesecake sit in the turned off pressure cooker for one hour. Carefully remove the lid and transfer the cheesecake from the cooker to the counter using the aluminum sling or rack. Let the cheesecake come to room temperature and then remove the foil from the top of the cake pan. Blot any liquid that might have condensed on the surface of the cake, wrap it in plastic wrap and refrigerate for at least 8 hours.

7. Before serving, make the dark chocolate ganache. Warm the heavy cream in small sauce pot until it simmers, but do not boil. Place the chocolate chips in large bowl and pour the warm cream on top. Whisk until chocolate chips are melted and smooth. Stir in the vanilla extract and let the ganache sit for 3 minutes.

8. Pour the ganache on top of the cheesecake and top with whole cherries. Let the cheesecake come to room temperature and let the ganache set before serving.

Index

A

Almonds
Chocolate Raspberry Almond Torte 212
Curried Carrot Soup 41
Quinoa Porridge 200
Quinoa Rice with Almonds 170
Roasted Red Pepper Aïoli 192

Anchovies
Farfalle Putanesca 54
Salmon Putanesca with White Beans 141

Apples
Curried Carrot Soup 41
Kielbasa with Sauerkraut and Apples 127
Maple Apple Blueberry Compote 209
Pork Stew with Cabbage and Tomatoes 123
Pot Roast Shoulder of Pork with Apple Gravy 126
Steel-Cut Oats with Apples and Raisins 201

Apricots
Madeira Ham with Apricots 128
Quinoa Porridge 200

Artichoke
Brown Rice Salad 176
Pork Chops with Artichokes 131
Steamed Artichokes with Dipping Sauces 190

Arugula
Farro Salad 166
Fusilli with Hot Italian Sausage 57

Asparagus
Vegetable Couscous 155

Avocado
Brown Rice Salad 176
Tortilla Soup 37

B

Bacon
Beets and Potatoes with Bacon 185
Breakfast Risotto 204
Hoppin' John 169
Loaded Baked Potato Soup 38
Penne Carbonara 63
Smoky Bacon Tomato Chickpeas 174

Bananas
Banana Cake with Chocolate Chunks 218
Blueberry Polenta with Bananas 203
Quinoa Porridge 200

Basil
Lemon-Basil Ricotta Dumplings 148
Vegetable Couscous 155

BBQ sauce
BBQ Turkey Mushroom Meatloaf 89

Beans
Beans, black
Black Bean and Mushroom Chili 44
Tortilla Soup 37
Beans, cannellini
Chipotle Pot Roast 113
Salmon Putanesca with White Beans 141
Beans, red kidney
Annie's Beef Chili 45
Chili Macaroni 59
Quinoa Chili with Kidney Beans and Corn 47
Tortilla Soup 37
Vegetable and Bean Stuffed Peppers 154
Beans, refried
Caribbean Pork Chil 42

Beef
Beef, brisket
Beef Brisket with Dried Plums, Cognac and Cream 94
Beef Brisket with Onion, Mushroom Gravy 92
Beef, chuck roast
Beef Dip Sandwiches 107
Chipotle Pot Roast 113
Beef, corned beef
Corned Beef Reuben Casserole 97
Jiggs Dinner 103
Beef, ground
Annie's Beef Chili 45
Chili Macaroni 59
Lamb Bolognese with Pistachio Gremolata 61
Parmesan Meatballs and Marinara 95
Sunday Gravy 69
Sweet Vidalia Onion Joes 100
Turkish Beef and Eggplant Moussaka 101
Beef, short ribs
Stout-Braised Beef Short Ribs 109
Beef, stew meat
Curried Beef with Cucumber Yogurt Sauce 110
Hunter's Beef Stew 104
Beef, top round
Beef Braciola with Mushrooms 98

Beer
Chipotle Pot Roast 113
Kielbasa with Sauerkraut and Apples 127
Stout-Braised Beef Short Ribs 109

Beets
Beetroot Bourguignon 163
Beets and Potatoes with Bacon 185

Bisquick mix
Chicken and Lemon-Chive Dumplings 72

Bitter greens
Lentil and Chickpea Stew, Spicy Bitter Greens 158

BJC FAV
Avglolemono with Chicken and Rice 32
BBQ Turkey Mushroom Meatloaf 89
Beets and Potatoes with Bacon 185
Blueberry Polenta with Bananas 203
Cauliflower with Lemon-Caper Vinaigrette 180
Chicken and Lemon-Chive Dumplings 72
Chicken Tikka Masala 85
Country Style Pork Ribs 122
Creamy Tomato Macaroni 52
Dry-Rubbed Baby Back Ribs with BBQ Sauce 119
Farro Salad 166
French Canadian Yellow Split Pea Soup 27
Jiggs Dinner 103
Lemon Oregano Chicken Breasts 81
Madeira Ham with Apricots 128
Mexican Brown Rice with Corn and Chilies 171
Parmesan Meatballs and Marinara 95
Pork Carnitas 125
Portobello Mushroom and Zucchini Moussaka 157
Pot Roast Shoulder of Pork 126
Provençal Fish Stew 134
Tortilla Soup 37
Veracruz Style Snapper with Rice 139

Blackberries
Blackberry Pear Compote 206
Blackberry Croissant Bread Pudding 216

Black-eyed Peas
Hoppin' John 169

Blueberries
Blueberry Polenta with Bananas 203
Lemon Blueberry Cheesecake 227
Maple Apple Blueberry Compote 209

Bourbon
Brown Sugar Bourbon Bread Pudding 217

Bread Pudding
Blackberry Croissant Bread Pudding 216
Brown Sugar Bourbon Bread Pudding 217

Breakfast
Blackberry Pear Compote 206
Blueberry Polenta with Bananas 203
Breakfast Risotto 204
Ham and Cheddar Grits 198
Maple Apple Blueberry Compote 209
Quinoa Porridge 200

Index

Steel-Cut Oats with Apples and Raisins 201
Strawberry Pomegranate Compote 208
Tropical Morning Rice Pudding 205

Broccoli
Broccoli Rice Casserole 149
Vegetable Coconut Curry 159
Vegetable Couscous 155

C

Cabbage
Corned Beef Reuben Casserole 97
Jiggs Dinner 103
Pork Stew with Cabbage and Tomatoes 123

Cake
Banana Cake with Chocolate Chunks 218
Carrot Cake with Cream Cheese Icing 220
Chocolate Raspberry Almond Torte 212
Pudding Chômeur 224

Capers
Cauliflower with Lemon-Caper Vinaigrette 180
Farfalle Putanesca 54
Pork Chops with Artichokes 131
Salmon Putanesca with White Beans 141
Tuna Caper Aïoli 192
Veracruz Style Snapper with Rice 139

Caramel
Crème Caramel with Orange and Hazelnuts 215

Carrots
Beetroot Bourguignon 163
Carrot Cake Rice Pudding 223
Carrot Cake with Cream Cheese Icing 220
Cumin Carrots with Kale 195
Curried Carrot Soup 41
Hunter's Beef Stew 104
Jiggs Dinner 103
Pork Chops with Orange Marmalade Glaze 116
Vegetable Coconut Curry 159

Cauliflower
Cauliflower Cheddar Soup 35
Cauliflower with Lemon-Caper Vinaigrette 180
Vegetable Coconut Curry 159

Cheese
Cheese, Asiago
Fusilli with Hot Italian Sausage 57
Cheese, Cheddar
Black Bean and Mushroom Chili 44
Breakfast Risotto 204
Broccoli Rice Casserole 149
Cauliflower Cheddar Soup 35
Chili Macaroni 59

Ham and Cheddar Grits 198
Loaded Baked Potato Soup 38
Pork Carnitas 125
Tortilla Soup 37
Vegetable and Bean Stuffed Peppers 154
Cheese, cream cheese
Carrot Cake Rice Pudding 223
Carrot Cake with Cream Cheese Icing 220
Cheese, feta
Greek Chicken and Potatoes 74
Lemon Oregano Chicken Breasts 81
Portobello Mushroom and Zucchini Moussaka 157
Roasted Red Pepper Rigatoni 64
Turkey Breast with Walnut Stuffing 86
Turkish Beef and Eggplant Moussaka 101
Vegetable Couscous 155
Cheese, Monterey Jack
Salsa Chicken Thighs with Rice 79
Cheese, Parmesan
Creamy Tomato Macaroni 52
Farfalle Putanesca 54
Lamb Bolognese with Pistachio Gremolata 61
Lemon-Basil Ricotta Dumplings 148
Penne Carbonara 63
Portobello Mushroom and Zucchini Moussaka 157
Potato Gratin 189
Risotto with Shiitake Mushrooms 146
Spaghetti Squash 152
Spinach Cheese Ravioli with Zucchini 55
Sunday Gravy 69
Turkey Bolognese Rigatoni 65
Turkey Tetrazzini 60
Cheese, Pecorino
Beef Braciola with Mushrooms 98
Penne Carbonara 63
Chesse, ricotta
Lemon-Basil Ricotta Dumplings 148

Cheesecake
Cherry Cheesecake with Ganache 231
Lemon Blueberry Cheesecake 227
Peanut Butter Cheesecake 228

Cherry
Cherry Cheesecake with Ganache 231
Dry-Rubbed Baby Back Ribs
  with Cherry Chipotle Sauce 120
Turkey Breast with Italian Sausage and Dried
  Cherry Stuffing 88

Chicken
Avglolemono with Chicken and Rice 32
Chicken and Corn Chowder 24
Chicken, breasts
Chicken and Lemon-Chive Dumplings 72
Chicken Marsala Stew 75
Chicken Pot Pie 82
Chicken Tikka Masala 85
Greek Chicken and Potatoes 74
Honey Mustard Chicken 76
Lemon Oregano Chicken Breasts 81
Chicken Noodle Soup 28
Chicken, thighs
Chicken Tikka Masala 85
Honey Mustard Chicken 76
Salsa Chicken Thighs with Rice 79
Tortilla Soup 37

Chickpeas
Annie's Beef Chili 45
Caribbean Pork Chili with Pineapple Salsa 42
Lentil and Chickpea Stew 158
Saffron Rice with Chickpeas 172
Smoky Bacon Tomato Chickpeas 174
Vegetable and Bean Stuffed Peppers 154

Chilies
Annie's Beef Chili 45
Black Bean and Mushroom Chili 44
Caribbean Pork Chili with Pineapple Salsa 42
Chile Verde 48
Quinoa Chili with Kidney Beans and Corn 47

Chocolate
Banana Cake with Chocolate Chunks 218
Brown Sugar Bourbon Bread Pudding 217
Cherry Cheesecake with Ganache 231
Chocolate Raspberry Almond Torte 212
Chocolate, white
White Chocolate Raspberry
  Rice Pudding 221
Peanut Butter Cheesecake 228

Clams
Cavatappi con Vongole 66

Coconut milk
Caribbean Pork Chili with Pineapple Salsa 42
Thai Coconut Mussels 142
Tropical Morning Rice Pudding 205
Vegetable Coconut Curry 159

Cognac
Beef Brisket with Dried Plums, Cognac
  and Cream 94

Index

Collard greens
Hoppin' John 169
Corn
Annie's Beef Chili 45
Chicken and Corn Chowder 24
Mexican Brown Rice with Corn and Chilies 171
Quinoa Chili with Kidney Beans and Corn 47
Vegetable and Bean Stuffed Peppers 154
Corned Beef
Corned Beef Reuben Casserole 97
Jiggs Dinner 103
Corn grits
Ham and Cheddar Grits 198
Lime Shrimp and Spicy Tomato Grits 137
Couscous
Vegetable Couscous 155
Cream
Beef Brisket with Dried Plums, Cognac
  and Cream 94
Curry
Curried Beef with Cucumber Yogurt Sauce 110
Curried Butternut Squash Pear Soup 29
Curried Carrot Soup 41
Vegetable Coconut Curry 159

D
Desserts
Banana Cake with Chocolate Chunks 218
Blackberry Croissant Bread Pudding 216
Brown Sugar Bourbon Bread Pudding 217
Carrot Cake Rice Pudding 223
Carrot Cake with Cream Cheese Icing 220
Cherry Cheesecake with Ganache 231
Chocolate Raspberry Almond Torte 212
Crème Caramel with Orange and Hazelnuts 215
Lemon Blueberry Cheesecake 227
Peanut Butter Cheesecake 228
Pudding Chômeur 224
White Chocolate Raspberry Rice Pudding 221

E
Edamame
Miso Brown Rice Bowl 151
Eggplant
Portobello Mushroom and Zucchini Moussaka 157
Turkish Beef and Eggplant Moussaka 101
Eggs
Breakfast Risotto 204

F
Farro
Farro Salad 166

Fennel
Provençal Fish Stew 134
Fish
Fish Facts 140
Fish, grouper
  Provençal Fish Stew 134
Fish, red snapper
  Provençal Fish Stew 134
  Veracruz Style Snapper with Rice 139
Fish, salmon
  Provençal Fish Stew 134
  Salmon Putanesca with White Beans 141
Flan
Crème Caramel with Orange and Hazelnuts 215

G
Ginger
Chicken Tikka Masala 85
Ginger Broth with Salmon and Shrimp 30
Grains and Beans
Brown Rice Salad with Artichoke Hearts 176
Farro Salad 166
Hoppin' John 169
Mexican Brown Rice with Corn and Chilies 171
Quinoa and Lentils with Mango and Mint 175
Quinoa Rice with Almonds 170
Saffron Rice with Chickpeas 172
Smoky Bacon Tomato Chickpeas 174
Spill the Beans 168
Grapes
Farro Salad 166

H
Ham
French Canadian Yellow Split Pea Soup 27
Ham and Cheddar Grits 198
Hoppin' John 169
Madeira Ham with Apricots 128
Hazelnuts
Crème Caramel with Orange and Hazelnuts 215
Farro Salad 166
Honey
Butternut Squash Purée 183
Honey Mustard Chicken 76
Pork Chops with Orange Marmalade Glaze 116
Horseradish
Beef Dip Sandwiches 107
Hunter's Beef Stew 104

K
Kale
Cumin Carrots with Kale 195
Kielbasa
Kielbasa with Sauerkraut and Apples 127
L
Lamb
Lamb Bolognese with Pistachio Gremolata 61
Leeks
Chicken Pot Pie with Leeks and Lemon 82
Roasted Red Pepper Rigatoni 64
Spaghetti Squash with Olive Marinara 152
Lemons
Avglolemono with Chicken and Rice 32
Cauliflower with Lemon-Caper Vinaigrette 180
Cavatappi con Vongole 66
Chicken and Lemon-Chive Dumplings 72
Chicken Pot Pie with Leeks and Lemon 82
Cumin Carrots with Kale 195
Lamb Bolognese with Pistachio Gremolata 61
Lemon-Basil Ricotta Dumplings 148
Lemon Blueberry Cheesecake 227
Lemon Oregano Chicken Breasts 81
Lentil and Chickpea Stew 158
Maple Apple Blueberry Compote 209
Pork Chops with Artichokes 131
Steamed Artichokes with Dipping Sauces 190
Strawberry Pomegranate Compote 208
Tuna Caper Aïoli 192
Turkey Breast with Walnut Stuffing 86
Vegetable Couscous 155
Lentils
Beetroot Bourguignon 163
Lentil and Chickpea Stew 158
Quinoa and Lentils with Mango and Mint 175
Spicy Quinoa and Red Lentil Soup 33
Limes
Caribbean Pork Chili with Pineapple Salsa 42
Lime Shrimp and Spicy Tomato Grits 137
Thai Coconut Mussels 142
Vegetable Coconut Curry 159
M
Mango
Quinoa and Lentils with Mango and Mint 175
Tropical Morning Rice Pudding 205
Maple syrup
Blueberry Polenta with Bananas 203
Creamy Maple Sweet Potatoes 182
French Canadian Yellow Split Pea Soup 27

Index

Maple Apple Blueberry Compote 209
Pudding Chômeur 224

Marmalade
Pork Chops with Orange Marmalade Glaze 116

Meatloaf
BBQ Turkey Mushroom Meatloaf 89

Mint
Quinoa and Lentils with Mango and Mint 175

Miso paste
Miso Brown Rice Bowl 151

Mushrooms
Annie's Beef Chili 45
BBQ Turkey Mushroom Meatloaf 89
Beef Braciola with Mushrooms 98
Beef Brisket with Onion and Mushroom Gravy 92
Beetroot Bourguignon 163
Black Bean and Mushroom Chili 44
Chicken Marsala Stew 75
Ginger Broth with Salmon and Shrimp 30
Hunter's Beef Stew 104
Portobello Mushroom and Zucchini Moussaka 157
Risotto with Shiitake Mushrooms 146
Turkey Tetrazzini 60

Mussels
Provençal Fish Stew 134
Thai Coconut Mussels 142

Mustard
Honey Mustard Chicken 76

O

Oats
Steel-Cut Oats with Apples and Raisins 201

Olives
Farfalle Putanesca 54
Fusilli with Hot Italian Sausage 57
Lemon Oregano Chicken Breasts 81
Salmon Putanesca with White Beans 141
Spaghetti Squash with Marinara 152
Veracruz Style Snapper with Rice 139

Onions
Beef Dip Sandwiches 107
Beetroot Bourguignon 163
Sweet Vidalia Onion Joes 100

Oranges
Blackberry Pear Compote 206
Butternut Squash Purée with Orange 183
Chipotle Orange Aïoli 192
Crème Caramel with Orange 215
Farro Salad 166
Honey Mustard Chicken 76

Pork Carnitas 125
Pork Chops with Orange Marmalade Glaze 116
Provençal Fish Stew 134

Orzo
Lemon Oregano Chicken Breasts with Orzo 81

P

Parsnips
Parsnip, Pear and Rosemary Mash 186

Pasta
Cavatappi con Vongole 66
Chicken Noodle Soup 28
Creamy Tomato Macaroni 52
Farfalle Putanesca 54
Fusilli with Hot Italian Sausage 57
Lamb Bolognese with Pistachio Gremolata 61
Pasta Primer 58
Penne Carbonara 63
Roasted Red Pepper Rigatoni 64
Spinach Cheese Ravioli with Zucchini 55
Sunday Gravy 69
Turkey Bolognese Rigatoni 65
Turkey Tetrazzini 60

Peanut Butter
Peanut Butter Cheesecake 228

Pears
Blackberry Pear Compote 206
Curried Butternut Squash Pear Soup 29
Parsnip, Pear and Rosemary Mash 186

Peas
Chicken Marsala Stew 75
Chicken Pot Pie with Leeks and Lemon 82
Risotto with Shiitake Mushrooms 146
Turkey Tetrazzini 60
Vegetable and Bean Stuffed Peppers 154

Pecans
Turkey Breast with Italian Sausage and Dried
  Cherry Stuffing 88

Peppers
Peppers, bell
  Annie's Beef Chili 45
  Caribbean Pork Chili with Pineapple Salsa 42
  Chili Macaroni 59
  Dry-Rubbed Baby Back Ribs with
    Sweet and Sour Sauce 120
  Greek Chicken and Potatoes 74
  Hoppin' John 169
  Hunter's Beef Stew 104
  Miso Brown Rice Bowl 151
  Quinoa Chili with Kidney Beans and Corn 47

Salsa Chicken Thighs with Rice 79
Sunday Gravy 69
Tortilla Soup 37
Vegetable and Bean Stuffed Peppers 154
  Vegetable Couscous 155

Peppers, Chipotle in Adobo
  Black Bean and Mushroom Chili 44
  Chipotle Orange Aïoli 192
  Chipotle Pot Roast 113
  Dry-Rubbed Baby Back Ribs with
    Cherry Chipotle Sauce 120

Peppers, Jalapeño
  Caribbean Pork Chili 42
  Chili Macaroni 59
  Lime Shrimp and Spicy Tomato Grits 137
  Mexican Brown Rice with Corn and Chilies 171
  Pork Carnitas 125
  Quinoa Chili with Kidney Beans and Corn 47
  Spicy Quinoa and Red Lentil Soup 33
  Tortilla Soup 37
  Veracruz Style Snapper with Rice 139

Peppers, Poblano
  Chile Verde 48
  Mexican Brown Rice with Corn and Chilies 171

Peppers, red chili
  Calamari Stew 136
  Spicy Quinoa and Red Lentil Soup 33
  Thai Coconut Mussels 142
  Vegetable Coconut Curry 159

Peppers, roasted red
  Roasted Red Pepper Aïoli 192
  Roasted Red Pepper Rigatoni 64

Pineapple
Caribbean Pork Chili with Pineapple Salsa 42
Dry-Rubbed Baby Back Ribs with Sweet
  and Sour Sauce 120
Tropical Morning Rice Pudding 205

Pinenuts
Beef Braciola with Mushrooms 98
Brown Rice Salad 176

Pistachios
Lamb Bolognese with Pistachio Gremolata 61

Plums
Beef Brisket with Dried Plums, Cognac
  and Cream 94

Polenta
Blueberry Polenta with Bananas 203

Pomegranate
Strawberry Pomegranate Compote 208

Index

Pork

Madeira Ham with Apricots 128

Pork, baby back ribs

Dry-Rubbed Baby Back Ribs
with BBQ Sauce 119

Dry-Rubbed Baby Back Ribs
with Cherry Chipotle Sauce 120

Pork, center cut chops

Pork Chops with Artichokes 131

Pork Chops with Orange Marmalade Glaze 116

Pork, country style ribs

Country Style Pork Ribs 122

Pork, ground

Parmesan Meatballs and Marinara 95

Pork, sausage

Fusilli with Hot Italian Sausage 57

Kielbasa with Sauerkraut and Apples 127

Pork, shoulder

Chile Verde 48

Pork Carnitas 125

Pork Stew with Cabbage and Tomatoes 123

Pot Roast Shoulder of Pork 126

Pork, stew meat

Caribbean Pork Chili 42

Sunday Gravy 69

Potatoes

Beetroot Bourguignon 163

Beets and Potatoes with Bacon 185

Butternut Squash Purée with Orange,Honey 183

Calamari Stew 136

Chicken and Lemon-Chive Dumplings 72

Chicken Marsala Stew 75

Curried Beef with Cucumber Yogurt Sauce 110

Greek Chicken and Potatoes 74

Honey Mustard Chicken with Orange and
Rosemary Potatoes 76

Jiggs Dinner 103

Loaded Baked Potato Soup 38

Potato Gratin 189

Pot Roast Shoulder of Pork 126

Provençal Fish Stew with Potatoes 134

Turkish Beef and Eggplant Moussaka 101

Vegetable Coconut Curry 159

Poultry

BBQ Turkey Mushroom Meatloaf 89

Chicken and Lemon-Chive Dumplings 72

Chicken Marsala Stew 75

Chicken Pot Pie with Leeks and Lemon 82

Chicken Tikka Masala 85

Greek Chicken and Potatoes 74

Honey Mustard Chicken 76

Lemon Oregano Chicken Breasts 81

Salsa Chicken Thighs with Rice 79

Turkey Breast with Italian Sausage and
Dried Cherry Stuffing 88

Turkey Breast with Spinach, Feta, Lemon
and Walnut Stuffing 86

Puff pastry

Chicken Pot Pie with Leeks and Lemon 82

Q

Quinoa

Quinoa and Lentils with Mango and Mint 175

Quinoa Chili with Kidney Beans and Corn 47

Quinoa Porridge 200

Quinoa Rice with Almonds 170

Spicy Quinoa and Red Lentil Soup 33

R

Raspberry

Chocolate Raspberry Almond Torte 212

White Chocolate Raspberry Rice Pudding 221

Rice

Avglolemono with Chicken and Rice 32

Breakfast Risotto 204

Broccoli Rice Casserole 149

Brown Rice Salad 176

Hoppin' John 169

Mexican Brown Rice with Corn and Chilies 171

Miso Brown Rice Bowl 151

Quinoa Rice with Almonds 170

Risotto with Shiitake Mushrooms, Butternut
Squash and Peas 146

Saffron Rice with Chickpeas 172

Salsa Chicken Thighs with Rice 79

Tropical Morning Rice Pudding 205

Veracruz Style Snapper with Rice 139

Rice Pudding

Carrot Cake Rice Pudding 223

Rosemary

Honey Mustard Chicken 76

Parsnip, Pear and Rosemary Mash 186

S

Saffron

Provençal Fish Stew 134

Saffron Rice with Chickpeas 172

Sauerkraut

Kielbasa with Sauerkraut and Apples 127

Sausage

Calamari Stew 136

Fusilli with Hot Italian Sausage 57

Sunday Gravy 69

Turkey Breast with Italian Sausage
and Dried Cherry Stuffing 88

Seafood

Calamari Stew 136

Ginger Broth with Salmon and Shrimp 30

Lime Shrimp and Spicy Tomato Grits 137

Provençal Fish Stew 134

Salmon Putanesca with White Beans 141

Thai Coconut Mussels 142

Veracruz Style Snapper with Rice 139

Sherry

Turkey Tetrazzini 60

Shrimp

Ginger Broth with Salmon and Shrimp 30

Lime Shrimp and Spicy Tomato Grits 137

Provençal Fish Stew 134

Snap peas

Pork Chops with Orange Marmalade Glaze 116

Soups

Avglolemono with Chicken and Rice 32

Cauliflower Cheddar Soup 35

Chicken and Corn Chowder 24

Chicken Noodle Soup 28

Curried Butternut Squash Pear Soup 29

Curried Carrot Soup 41

French Canadian Yellow Split Pea Soup 27

Ginger Broth with Salmon and Shrimp 30

Loaded Baked Potato Soup 38

Spicy Quinoa and Red Lentil Soup 33

Tortilla Soup 37

Spinach

Turkey Breast with Spinach, Feta, Lemon
and Walnut Stuffing 86

Vegetable Coconut Curry 159

Split peas

French Canadian Yellow Split Pea Soup 27

Jiggs Dinner 103

Squash

Butternut Squash Purée with Orange
and Honey 183

Curried Butternut Squash Pear Soup 29

Risotto with Shiitake Mushrooms, Butternut
Squash and Peas 146

Spaghetti Squash with Marinara 152

Vegetable Couscous 155

Squid

Calamari Stew 136

Strawberries

Strawberry Pomegranate Compote 208

Index

Super Easy

Avglolemono with Chicken and Rice 32

Beef Brisket with Dried Plums, Cognac
and Cream 94

Beef Dip Sandwiches 107

Broccoli Rice Casserole 149

Butternut Squash Purée with Orange
and Honey 183

Cauliflower with Lemon-Caper Vinaigrette 180

Cavatappi con Vongole 66

Chicken Tikka Masala 85

Chile Verde 48

Creamy Maple Sweet Potatoes 182

Creamy Tomato Macaroni 52

Cumin Carrots with Kale 195

Curried Butternut Squash Pear Soup 29

Farfalle Putanesca 54

French Canadian Yellow Split Pea Soup 27

Ham and Cheddar Grits 198

Honey Mustard Chicken with Orange
and Rosemary Potatoes 76

Kielbasa with Sauerkraut and Apples 127

Lemon Oregano Chicken Breasts with Orzo,
Olives and Feta Cheese 81

Loaded Baked Potato Soup 38

Madeira Ham with Apricots 128

Parmesan Meatballs and Marinara 95

Parsnip, Pear and Rosemary Mash 186

Penne Carbonara 63

Quinoa and Lentils with Mango and Mint 175

Quinoa Porridge with Banana, Apricots
and Almonds 200

Quinoa Rice with Almonds 170

Risotto with Shiitake Mushrooms,
Butternut Squash and Peas 146

Roasted Red Pepper Rigatoni with Feta Cheese 64

Saffron Rice with Chickpeas 172

Salmon Putanesca with White Beans 141

Salsa Chicken Thighs with Rice 79

Spicy Quinoa and Red Lentil Soup 33

Spinach Cheese Ravioli with Zucchini
and Marinara 55

Steamed Artichokes with Dipping Sauces 190

Steel-Cut Oats with Apples and Raisins 201

Strawberry Pomegranate Compote 208

Tropical Morning Rice Pudding 205

Vegetable and Bean Stuffed Peppers
with Marinara 154

Sweet potatoes

Creamy Maple Sweet Potatoes 182

T

Tofu

Miso Brown Rice Bowl 151

Tomatoes

Annie's Beef Chili 45

Beef Braciola with Mushrooms 98

Black Bean and Mushroom Chili 44

Breakfast Risotto 204

Brown Rice Salad 176

Calamari Stew 136

Caribbean Pork Chili with Pineapple Salsa 42

Cavatappi con Vongole 66

Chicken Tikka Masala 85

Chili Macaroni 59

Chipotle Pot Roast 113

Creamy Tomato Macaroni 52

Curried Beef with Cucumber Yogurt Sauce 110

Farfalle Putanesca 54

Fusilli with Hot Italian Sausage, Tomatoes,
Arugula and Black Olives 57

Greek Chicken and Potatoes 74

Hunter's Beef Stew 104

Lamb Bolognese with Pistachio Gremolata 61

Lemon-Basil Ricotta Dumplings 148

Lemon Oregano Chicken Breasts 81

Lentil and Chickpea Stew 158

Lime Shrimp and Spicy Tomato Grits 137

Mexican Brown Rice with Corn and Chilies 171

Parmesan Meatballs and Marinara 95

Pork Chops with Artichokes 131

Pork Stew with Cabbage and Tomatoes 123

Portobello Mushroom and Zucchini Moussaka 157

Provençal Fish Stew 134

Quinoa Chili with Kidney Beans and Corn 47

Roasted Red Pepper Rigatoni 64

Salmon Putanesca with White Beans 141

Smoky Bacon Tomato Chickpeas 174

Spaghetti Squash with Marinara 152

Spinach Cheese Ravioli with Zucchini 55

Stout-Braised Beef Short Ribs 109

Sunday Gravy 69

Sweet Vidalia Onion Joes 100

Tortilla Soup 37

Turkey Bolognese Rigatoni 65

Turkish Beef and Eggplant Moussaka 101

Vegetable Coconut Curry 159

Vegetable Couscous 155

Veracruz Style Snapper with Rice 139

Tuna

Tuna Caper Aïoli 192

Turkey

BBQ Turkey Mushroom Meatloaf 89

Turkey Breast with Italian Sausage
and Dried Cherry Stuffing 88

Turkey Breast with Spinach, Feta, Lemon
and Walnut Stuffing 86

Turkey Tetrazzini 60

V

Vegetable Main Dishes

Beetroot Bourguignon 163

Broccoli Rice Casserole 149

Lemon-Basil Ricotta Dumplings 148

Lentil and Chickpea Stew 158

Miso Brown Rice Bowl 151

Portobello Mushroom and Zucchini Moussaka 157

Risotto with Shiitake Mushrooms,
Butternut Squash and Peas 146

Spaghetti Squash with Leek
and Olive Marinara 152

Vegetable and Bean Stuffed Peppers
with Marinara 154

Vegetable Coconut Curry 159

Vegetable Couscous with Tomatoes,
Feta and Basil 155

Vegetable Side Dishes

Beets and Potatoes with Bacon 185

Butternut Squash Purée with Orange
and Honey 183

Cauliflower with Breadcrumbs and
Lemon-Caper Vinaigrette 180

Chipotle Orange Aïoli 192

Creamy Maple Sweet Potatoes 182

Cumin Carrots with Kale 195

Parsnip, Pear and Rosemary Mash 186

Potato Gratin 189

Roasted Red Pepper Aïoli 192

Steamed Artichokes with Dipping Sauces 190

Tuna Caper Aïoli 192

Vegetarian

Beetroot Bourguignon with Fingerling Potatoes
and Lentils 163

Black Bean and Mushroom Chili 44

Blackberry Pear Compote 206

Blueberry Polenta with Bananas 203

Broccoli Rice Casserole 149

Brown Rice Salad with Artichoke Hearts,
Avocado and Pinenuts 176

Index

Vegetarian (continued)

Butternut Squash Purée with Orange
and Honey 183

Cauliflower Cheddar Soup 35

Cauliflower with Breadcrumbs and
Lemon-Caper Vinaigrette 180

Chipotle Orange Aïoli 192

Creamy Maple Sweet Potatoes 182

Creamy Tomato Macaroni 52

Cumin Carrots with Kale 195

Curried Carrot Soup with Apple
and Almond Topping 41

Farro Salad with Hazelnuts, Arugula
and Grapes 166

Lemon-Basil Ricotta Dumplings 148

Lentil and Chickpea Stew
with Spicy Bitter Greens 158

Maple Apple Blueberry Compote 209

Mexican Brown Rice with Corn and Chilies 171

Miso Brown Rice Bowl with Tofu
and Edamame 151

Parsnip, Pear and Rosemary Mash 186

Portobello Mushroom and Zucchini Moussaka 157

Potato Gratin 189

Quinoa and Lentils with Mango and Mint 175

Quinoa Chili with Kidney Beans and Corn 47

Quinoa Porridge with Banana, Apricots
and Almonds 200

Quinoa Rice with Almonds 170

Risotto with Shiitake Mushrooms,
Butternut Squash and Peas 146

Roasted Red Pepper Aïoli 192

Roasted Red Pepper Rigatoni
with Feta Cheese 64

Saffron Rice with Chickpeas 172

Spaghetti Squash with Leek
and Olive Marinara 152

Spicy Quinoa and Red Lentil Soup 33

Spinach Cheese Ravioli with Zucchini
and Marinara 55

Steamed Artichokes with Dipping Sauces 190

Steel-Cut Oats with Apples and Raisins 201

Strawberry Pomegranate Compote 208

Tropical Morning Rice Pudding 205

Vegetable and Bean Stuffed Peppers
with Marinara 154

Vegetable Coconut Curry 159

Vegetable Couscous with Tomatoes,
Feta and Basil 155

W

Walnuts

Turkey Breast with Spinach, Feta, Lemon
and Walnut Stuffing 86

Wine

Beetroot Bourguignon 163

Calamari Stew 136

Chicken Marsala Stew 75

Lemon-Basil Ricotta Dumplings 148

Madeira Ham with Apricots 128

Pork Chops with Artichokes 131

Pot Roast Shoulder of Pork with Apple Gravy 126

Provençal Fish Stew 134

Risotto with Shiitake Mushrooms 146

Salmon Putanesca with White Beans 141

Thai Coconut Mussels 142

Turkey Breast with Italian Sausage
and Dried Cherry Stuffing 88

Veracruz Style Snapper with Rice 139

Y

Yogurt

Chicken Tikka Masala 85

Curried Beef with Cucumber Yogurt Sauce 110

Z

Zucchini

Portobello Mushroom and Zucchini Moussaka 157

Spinach Cheese Ravioli with Zucchini
and Marinara 55

Turkish Beef and Eggplant Moussaka 101

Vegetable Couscous 155

Tip Index

Allspice, about 223

Anchovies, storing and uses 54

Artichokes, how to eat 190

Bananas, how to ripen 218

Beef Information 108

Bitter greens, about 158

Bourbon, substitution 217

Brown rice, about 171

Chicken Information 80

Clarified butter, how to make your own 160

Corn, cutting kernels off the cob 47

Country style ribs, about 122

Crème Fraîche, into whipping cream 212

Fish Information 140

Foaming, using butter or oil to control 201

Ginger, freezing 30

Grains and Beans Information 168

Jalapeño peppers, about 125

Leeks, cleaning 64

Maple Syrup, about 224

Marsala wine, about 75

Miso, about 151

Pasta Information 58

Pears, how to ripen 206

Pomegranate, seeding 166

Pork Information 121

Portobello mushrooms, preparing 44

Sherry, about 60

Vegetable Information 193

Cooking Charts

	Cooking Time HIGH pressure (minutes)	Liquid Needed	Release Method		Cooking Time HIGH pressure (minutes)	Liquid Needed	Release Method
Poultry							
Chicken Bones for stock	40	6 cups	NATURAL	Chicken Thigh (boneless)	4	1 cup	QUICK
Chicken Breast (bone in)	6	1 cup	QUICK	Chicken, Whole	20	1½ cups	NATURAL
Chicken Breast (boneless)	4	1 cup	QUICK	Cornish Game Hen (1 to 1½ pounds)	8	1 cup	NATURAL
Chicken Thigh (bone in)	7	1 cup	QUICK	Turkey Breast (boneless, 2 to 3 pounds)	20 to 25	1½ cups	NATURAL
Beef							
Beef Bones for stock	40	6 cups	NATURAL	Meatloaf	35	1½ cups	NATURAL
Brisket (3½ to 4 pounds)	55 to 65	1½ cups	NATURAL	Pot Roast (3½ to 4 pounds)	55 to 65	2 cups	NATURAL
Corned Beef Brisket	55	covered	NATURAL	Short Ribs	55	1½ cups	NATURAL
Flank Steak (1 pound)	25	1 cup	NATURAL	Stew Meat (1-inch cubes)	15 to 20	1 cup	NATURAL
Ground Beef	5	1 cup	QUICK	Veal Shanks	20 to 25	1½ cups	NATURAL
Meatballs	5	1 cup	NATURAL	Veal Stew Meat (1-inch cubes)	10	1 cup	NATURAL
Pork							
Baby Back Ribs	30	1 cup	NATURAL	Pork Chops (boneless, 1-inch)	4 to 5	1½ cups	NATURAL
Country Style Ribs	20 to 25	1½ cups	NATURAL	Pork Loin (2 to 2½ pounds)	25	1½ cups	NATURAL
Ground Pork	5	1 cup	QUICK	Pork Shoulder (3 pounds)	55	1½ cups	NATURAL
Ham (bone in, 5 pounds, pre-cooked)	25 to 30	1½ cups	NATURAL	Sausages	10 to 15	1½ cups	QUICK
				Spare Ribs	45	1 cup	NATURAL
Meatballs	5	1 cup	NATURAL	Stew Meat (1-inch cubes)	15 to 20	1 cup	NATURAL
Pork Chops (bone in, 1-inch)	6	1½ cups	NATURAL				
Lamb							
Ground Lamb	5	1 cup	QUICK	Leg of Lamb (boneless, 3½ to 4 pounds)	35 to 45	1½ cups	NATURAL
Lamb Shanks	30	1½ cups	NATURAL	Stew Meat (1-inch cubes)	15 to 20	1 cup	NATURAL
Meatballs	5	1 cup	NATURAL				
Fish and Seafood							
Calamari	20	5 cup	QUICK	Mussels	4	2 cup	QUICK
Clams	4	1 cup	QUICK	Salmon	5	4 cup	QUICK
Crab Legs	4	1 cup	QUICK	Shrimp	2	3 cup	QUICK
Fish Fillet (1-inch thick)	5	6 cup	QUICK				

Cooking Charts

	Cooking Time HIGH pressure (minutes)	Liquid Needed	Release Method		Cooking Time HIGH pressure (minutes)	Liquid Needed	Release Method
Grains (1 cup)							
Barley (pearled)	20 to 25	3 cups	QUICK	**Poletna** (fine, not instant)	5	4 cups	QUICK
Brown Rice	20	2 cups	NATURAL	**Quinoa**	5	1½ cups	QUICK
Bulgur	6	2 cups	QUICK	**Steel Cut Oats**	5	3 cups	NATURAL
Farro (pearled)	8	2 cups	QUICK	**White Rice, long-grain**	4 to 6	1½ cups	QUICK
Farro (whole grain)	18	3 cups	QUICK	**White Rice, short-grain**	7	2⅔ cups	QUICK
Polenta (coarse, not instant)	8 to 10	4 cups	QUICK	**Wild Rice**	22	3 to 4 cups	QUICK

	Un-Soaked	Soaked or Quick-Soaked			Un-Soaked	Soaked or Quick-Soaked	
Beans and Legumes							
Black Beans	25	7	NATURAL	**Kidney Beans**	25	8 to 10	NATURAL
Black-Eyed Peas	8	6	NATURAL	**Lentils**	7 to 8	unnecessary	QUICK
Cannellini Beans	25	7	NATURAL	**Navy Beans**	20	8 to 10	NATURAL
Chickpeas	35 to 40	15	NATURAL	**Pinto Beans**	25	8 to 10	NATURAL
Great Northern Beans	25	8 to 10	NATURAL	**Split Peas**	8 to 10	unnecessary	NATURAL
				White Beans	20	8 to 10	NATURAL

Vegetables							
Acorn Squash (halved)	8	1 cup	QUICK	**Eggplant**	3 to 4	1 cup	QUICK
Artichokes (medium, whole)	12	1 cup	QUICK	**Fennel** (wedges)	4	1 cup	QUICK
Asparagus	2	1 cup	QUICK	**Green Beans**	3 to 4	1 cup	QUICK
Beets (medium, whole)	15	1 cup	QUICK	**Kale**	4	1 cup	QUICK
Broccoli	3	1 cup	QUICK	**Leeks** (1-inch pieces)	4	1 cup	QUICK
Broccoli Rabe	3	1 cup	QUICK	**Parsnips** (1-inch chunks)	4 to 5	1 cup	QUICK
Brussels Sprouts	4 to 6	1 cup	QUICK	**Potatoes** (1-inch chunks or small whole)	6 to 8	1 cup	QUICK
Butternut Squash (1-inch cubes)	5	1 cup	QUICK	**Rutabaga** (1-inch chunks)	4	1 cup	QUICK
Cabbage (quartered)	4 to 6	1 cup	QUICK	**Spaghetti Squash** (halved)	12 to 15	1 cup	QUICK
Beets (medium, whole)	15	1 cup	QUICK	**Sweet Potatoes** (1-inch chunks)	4 to 5	1 cup	QUICK
Cauliflower (whole)	12 to 15	1 cup	QUICK	**Swiss Chard**	2	1 cup	QUICK
Collard Greens	5 to 10	1 cup	QUICK	**Turnips** (1-inch chunks)	3 to 4	1 cup	QUICK
Corn on the Cob	2 to 3	1 cup	QUICK				